MY HOUSE TO YOURS

How to Look Younger,

Feel Better, and

Live a Happier Life

D0873128

Doris B. Gill

Copyright © 1987 by Doris B. Gill

All rights reserved. No part of this book may be used or reproduced in any manner whatsoever without written permission except in brief passages embodied in critical articles and reviews. For information write to:
Crab Cove Books,
P.O. Box 214
Alameda, California 94501

First Printing 1987

Printed in The United States of America

ISBN: 0-9618693-1-3
Library of Congress Catalog Card Number: 87-71395

Typography by: BookPrep,
            1630 Salem Drive,
            Gilroy, California 95020

This book is for educational and informational purposes only, and in no way is intended to substitute advise from a physican. Although possible dosage is discussed, this book is not intended to be medical advice.

ACKNOWLEDGEMENT

In appreciation of your support, all you have taught me, and from the pleasure of just knowing you.

Elizabeth Lodge Rees, M.D., F.A.A.P.
Rachael M. Lombardo, D.C.
Dr. Yu Chen, M.D. of China
Dr. Yun Hsieh M.D. of China
Grayce LeFord Guyer Robbins
Melissa Blanton

Dedicated to my family

Susan Marie & Rick
Derek & David

Steven Kent & Dani
Dannon & Trayce

Jeffrey Bruce & Dege
Baby Sierra

Kevin Scott

TABLE OF CONTENTS

PREFACE

Imagine you have come to my house for a visit. We are sitting in comfortable chairs in front of a cozy fire. We are sipping a cup of aromatic tea as we talk. Perhaps you are a teenager with acne, or a women going through menapause or having a weight problem. Maybe you are a bachelor and need some help with your laundry stains, or a young parent who has not defined your philosophy for raising children, or who has a baby that is not sleeping all night. Perhaps you would only like to know how to get last years Poinsettia to bloom again this holiday season.

No matter who you are, or on what "arc of the circle" you are living, this book should help improve the quality of your life, and your family's life too. Just think of this book as a silent friend in your home, only giving advise when asked, someone you can call upon to solve many of life's problems and challenges.

If you are a parent, or if you are responsible for the health and welfare of others, this book can make life easier and a lot more fun. Read on, even if you have only yourself to consider, and would like to improve the quality of your life.

It has always bothered me to see people suffering when there are so many simple remedies that can provide relief and increase comfort. There are also many simple things we can do to improve the quality of our health and life in general.

If you had worldy riches, a great love, academic degrees, or a chance to travel the world over, these things could not be used or enjoyed to the fullest without good health.

"We are what we eat" really is a fact. Most all of our ills are the result of our bodies, or our ancestors' bodies, being "short changed." Properly-balanced fuel to run without "knocking" was not provided. No matter what the complaint, either serious or minor, good nutrition can help.

The following hints and suggestions are not meant to be a substitute for sound, professional, medical advice. They may help to improve health without dangerous drugs. Drugs can often have side effects that we are not even made aware of.

Also included are some "slices of life" or vignettes, along with healthful as well as helpful hints.

This little book is the result of many years of study including articles, publications, and books written by doctors, nutritionists, and health practitioners who believe in preventive medicine and natural cures. My French Grandmother has been the source of many of these remedies, and the experience of raising my four children has been most helpful.

Theories come and theories go, but all the remedies included have been proven and used by many people with much success. I would like to share them with you.

I. FAVORS

Do Yourself A Favor

It may seem like an enormous chore to drastically change your life style to a more healthy way of living. Even if you are well motivated, it can be very confusing. Where do we begin? How do we make the change? Here are some simple ways to start:

Reduce Refined Sugar

If you decided to do just one thing to improve your health, giving up refined sugar could be the most significant.

Sugar causes many horrible diseases, including diabetes, arthritis, bursitis, neuritis, rheumatism, digestive track problems, arterioslerosis, and heart disease, just to name a few. It clogs your arteries and robs you of precious vitamins and minerals.

Sugar causes a vicious circle - the more you get, the more you crave as your body cries out for all those deficient nutrients.

We were brain-washed by the sugar industry for so long that we believed we needed sugar for "energy." It is now believed that this is not true. There is natural sugar in many foods we eat every day.

If you want an energy lift, try a small handful of raisins to raise your blood sugar. Mix them with raw sunflower seeds or nuts to keep your blood sugar from dropping. Keep these seeds and nuts in the freezer to preserve their freshness and prevent them from becoming rancid. Use raw honey as a sweetener if desired, but try to reduce all sweetener intake.

Giving up sugar doesn't mean you can't have an occasional

sweet. Just don't get back into the habit of eating sugar products all the time. Of course, it would be better if you gave up these products altogether. Once you rid yourself of the sugar habit and are healthier, you probably won't even wish to eat sweets because of the body reactions. You may feel nauseated or have a rapid heartbeat after ingesting sugar.

Drink Natural Liquids (Soft Drinks vs. Real Drinks)

If you think about it, we are spending money for completely non-nutritive products full of chemicals, artificial sweeteners, or loaded with sugar. One leading soft drink has nine teaspoons of sugar to each serving!

Have you ever really listened to the words of some of those "pop" commercials? They are spectacular, sensational, and cost a fortune, but they don't say anything about the soft drink, because there isn't anything good to say. They are selling the "sizzle," not the "steak."

Even among children, liver damage has dramatically increased in the last few years. One of the reasons is the high consumption of soft drinks.

There are so many other things to drink. Just plain old water tastes awfully good when you are thirsty. I prefer filtered water and try to drink several glasses every day.

If you do use filtered, or bottled water be sure that it is from a reputable company.

There are also many good, naturally sweetened, fruit juices. You can squeeze fresh oranges or put fresh strawberries and pineapple in the blender with ice cubes. Yogurt may be added. You may want to make enough to freeze some for "fruitcicles." (See Over Weight.)

Herbal teas are also good. In addition to the medicinal varieties, there are other flavorful teas nice enough to serve guests. Many of them make delicious iced drinks too. I don't keep soft drinks, coffee, or regular tea in my home anymore. Some of my favorite herb teas are: Spearmint, Comfrey

Peppermint, Lemon Grass, Almond, Orange Cinnamon, Sleepy Time, and Red Zinger, to name a few. Check your supermarket or health food store for many others. Remember to read the labels to see that you are getting only herbs.

When dining out, take herbal teas in a plastic bag to enjoy after your meal instead of coffee or soft drinks. Take enough to offer your dinner companions. I've done this on airplanes, and my seat mate is usually delighted and surprised at how good the tea is.

Eat Foods That Are Alive.

Shun dead, processed foods. Try to get fresh, raw, fruits and vegetables at each meal. Start your repast with things like radishes, cucumber slices, celery, and carrot sticks. End the meal with fresh pineapple, melon, orange, or grapefuit slices.

Don't eat the same foods every day. Get a variety. You can become allergic to any food you eat too often. Your vegetables can be eaten raw, steamed, or baked to preserve all the goodness. Boiling washes away many of the nutrients.

It may take a little longer to prepare food in this manner but it will be beneficial to you and your family.

Chew your food slowly and thoroughly. Be relaxed. Put down your fork between bites. Don't eat if you are upset. Really taste and relish each morsel without rushing. Don't read or watch TV - just concentrate on eating. This will help you feel more satisfied.

You may have to visit your grocery store more often. If you can spare the time, shop like the Europeans do. They do their marketing daily, buying only fresh foods for that day's meals.

Put on your blinders when you pass the processed foods. If you wish to consider these foods, then read the labels. You will see many of the items aren't real food at all and the labels read like a chemistry exam.

Buy whole grained breads. I keep mine in the freezer

because I don't use it very fast.

Select enough quantity and variety of fresh fruits and vegetables to last only a couple of days. Don't buy so much that they will spoil or lose their freshness.

Purchase chicken, turkey, fish, and, if you still eat red meat, buy only lean cuts and trim every bit of visible fat.

Stock up on a variety of grains and beans, includng brown rice (keep it refrigerated or in the freezer), and lentils.

Use non-fat milk and low-fat yogurt. Avoid saturated fats like margarine, lard, meat fats, hydrogenated peanut butter, and processed cheese. To cut down on butter consumption, try natural peanut butter on morning toast. Use cold pressed vegetable oils like sunflower, safflower, or peanut oil for salads and cooking. Keep the oils tightly closed and always store in the refrigerator. Remember that these oils have the same amount of calories as other fats (100 calories per tablespoon).

By eating foods that are not processed, you'll be surprised at how much money you will save, and your body will repay you by performing better.

Get Nitrites & Nitrates Out of Your Diet

By giving up wieners, sausages, bacon, and ham you could reduce your chances of getting cancer of the lower digestive tract. If you have arthritis, bursites, or rheumatism, it will help improve your condition if you eliminate the nitrites and nitrates in your diet. Pork also aggravates these conditions.

Find A Good Nutritionist

Find a good nutritionist to help you plan what foods, vitamins, minerals, and diet are best for you. This will take the guess work out of your nutritional needs.

A specialist can tell a lot by looking at your fingernails, tongue, eyes, skin, and muscle tone. He or she will probably ask questions about your diet and health habits.

Start by making a list of the foods you eat, any health problems or complaints, and any questions you want answered. He or she may take a hair sample for testing of your mineral balance and to see if you have any toxic metals like mercury, lead, cadmium, or aluminum.

I have a wonderful nutritionist who is also an M.D. and provides me with professional guidance.

At the age of 45, a woman friend of mine ended up in the hospital because she couldn't breathe. She kept having attacks, and the more she worried about it, the more severe they were. The internist that examined her could find no reason for her breathing problem and told her it was probably nerves. She seemed to get weaker and weaker.

I suggested she see my nutritionist, who took a hair sample and found that my friend's calcium was too high and that her potassium and magnesium were too low. She had mercury and lead poisoning also.

It so happened, my friend had been taking a calcium suupplement of 12 bone meal tablets a day for a back problem. It had helped her back, but she had really thrown her electolites off and possibly gotten the mercury and lead poison from a poor source of bone meal.

She never related her poor health to taking the bone meal and probably would have died if she hadn't seen the nutritionist, who put her on potassium, magnesium, and manganese supplements. It took several years before my friend was restored to good health. Needless to say, she never takes anything new in the way of supplements without checking with this nutritionist.

Acupuncture Can Help

Acupuncture is frequently helpful for many ailments and pain, but be sure that you find a doctor with good credentials and that sterile needles are used.

This ancient Chinese science has been used for centuries

to cure ailments and relieve pain. (I know of no side effects.) This treatment includes the use of many herbs. In modern times, the Japanese have enhanced accupuncture with electricity, which makes the needles even more effective.

My acupuncturist was a surgeon in China for nine years before coming to the United States. In addition to her practice, she is a professor at an accredited acupuncture college. She and her husband are both very dedicated doctors, and I feel very fortunate to have found them.

I have personally seen some astounding results from the use of accupuncture. I will relate a few of them to you:

1. A 13 year old girl with an acute hearing problem since birth was able to use the phone for the first time after only four treatments.

2. A heroin addict was able to stop using drugs after two treatments. His only discomfort was joint pain and some trouble sleeping. These symptoms were gone after a few more visits.

3. A stroke victim went from a wheelchair to a walker after only eight treatments.

4. Several childless couples now have babies. The wives became pregnant after eight to ten visits.

5. A man with low blood sugar had no more problems after four visits.

6. Many physicans with back, knee, or neck injuries are turning to accupuncture as an alternative to their own traditional treatments.

7. Weight loss without discomfort or dieting has been ac-

complished by many men and women. They have lost as much as 30 or 40 pounds.

Take Responsibility For Your Own Health

Take as much responsibility for your own health as you can. You can do this in many ways. Here are a few suggestions:

1. Read books and articles by qualified practitioners on nutrition and the interaction of vitamins, minerals, and hormones in your body.

    A good place to start is any of the Adele Davis books such as "Let's Get Well", "Let's Have Healthy Children", or "Let's Cook It Right". They are published by Signet Books and can be found in most book stores and health food stores. They are wonderful reference books. I refer to them often.

    Two books in the Prevention Total Health System series are "Understanding Vitamins and Minerals" and "Fighting Disease", both by the Editors of Prevention Magazine, Rodale Press, Emmaus, Pa. 18048. They are well written, illustrated, easy to understand, and fascinating.

2. Read labels on foods, cosmetics, toothpaste - anything you use on or in your body. After you do your reading, you will know what to look for.

3. Remove all aluminum from your kitchen including foil, strainers, measuring cups, spoons, and pots and pans. Many foods react chemically when they come in contact with aluminum. Also be sure that aluminum derivitives are not included in your hand and body lotion or deodorant. If you use baking powder, choose one that does not contain aluminum.

4. Prevent deterioration of foods. Poultry and fish start

deteriorating in less than twenty minutes if left unre-
frigerated. So it is a good idea to do your defrosting in the
microwave or in the refrigerator. When you have a buffet
or picnic, see that *all* your food is on ice or kept heated. It
is especially important to keep salads cold if they
contain mayonnaise or eggs.

Breadboards, cutting boards, and can openers are a
real breeding ground for bacteria. They should be
cleaned after each use. Scrub thoroughly with a brush
and hot soapy water.

5.   When a medication is prescribed, ask your doctor about
side effects and what other alternatives you may have.

Once a young friend took a medication for a bladder
infection while pregnant. When her baby's first teeth
came in, they were all brown! No one warned her that
this could happen from an antibiotic. Luckily his perma-
nent teeth were fine.

6.   Find a good nutritionist. (As previously mentioned).
This could be the most important step to wellness if you
follow his or her advice.

7.   Make sure your hands are clean. It is now believed that
more colds and viruses are contracted from shaking
hands and touching door knobs and then touching the
mouth, scratching the nose, or rubbing the eyes, than
any other way. Try to keep your hands away from your
face. It seems to be a nervous habit with most people.
Wash your hands frequently.

Carry towelettes when away from home. They are
handy to use after handling a menu in a restaurant, using
a public restroom, or shaking hands before eating.

Eat Less

Forget your membership in the "Clean Plate Club." Stop

eating before you feel full. It takes 20 minutes for your brain to tell your stomach it has had enough.

Overeating is very hard on tissues, arteries, kidneys, digestive track, and lungs. It sets up your body for chronic diseases.

Here are a few suggestions to retard your appetite:

1. Have a tablespoon of cold pressed peanut oil before eating. The oil stays in your stomach longer than other foods and gives you a feeling of being full.

2. Take a 1,500 mg. garlic tablet with each meal. It will reduce your appetite and is also very good for you. You will probably find that there is no offensive odor.

3. If you do feel hungry between meals, take a small bite (1/2 teaspoon) of natural peanut butter, or a tablespoon of raw sunflower seeds. Sometimes you think you are hungry when all you really need is more water.

    Try to drink several glasses of water each day, but don't drink for an hour before or after each meal. Liquids tend to dellute digestive enzymes.

4. Here is something I found by accident that reduces the appetite. Break open a garlic tablet and dab a little of the oil directly under or in your nose. This works very well, but you may want to try it when you are at home alone.

5. If watching TV causes you to overeat, find something else to do with your evenings. Play board games with your family or friends, take a class, or turn on the radio and start a project that you've been putting off. Eating after 6 P.M. is the worst time, because you don't burn up the calories before going to sleep.

Stop Smoking

Run, don't walk, to the nearest ashtray. Put out that last cigarette. If you can't quit by yourself, get help. Acupuncture works very well for most people I know who have tried it. Smell a dirty ashtray when you crave a weed, and think of how your "black" lungs are turning pink and healthy.

I smoked for many years, and here are some of the things that resulted, either directly or indirectly from my smoking.

a) All four of my babies were born prematurely by: 17 days, 21 days, 33 days, and 17 days.

b) Three of my babies had hernias. One child was only four weeks old when the hernia was discovered.

c) Obstructions of blood vessels in my young son's kidneys resulted in three serious surgeries. He had only one testicle along with a double hernia.

d) Broken blood vessels in my face.

e) Loss of energy. I noticed a dramatic increase in energy when I stopped smoking.

f) All three of my sons smoked at one time, however; only one smokes now. They were emulating their mother.

If you are already a non-smoker, or intend to become one, make a consious effort to be in a smoke-free environment. This is doubly important if you are trying to quit, because the sooner you rid your body of nicotine, the sooner the withdrawal symtoms will recede. Try to associate with non-smokers, and don't be afraid to let your smoking friends know

your plan. (They will probably admire your will power.) With
fewer and fewer smokers all the time, it should be easier to
find friends who don't have this dirty habit. When making out
party invitation lists, think of inviting only non-smokers. Only
patronize restaurants that have non-smoking sections. Let
the proprietor know why you won't make a return visit until
you can eat without smoke as a side dish. If enough people do
this, restauranteers will soon get the message. After all, they
are interested in pleasing the majority and having a full house
too.

Imagery Is a Powerful Tool
   The mind is a very powerful tool and can be used in many
positive ways. Listed below are a few suggestions on how to
use your imagination to improve your life style.

1.   If you have an important interview or meeting, do the
     following for several nights before the big day: When you
     go to bed, relax your whole body. Start with your head.
     Relax your face, then your jaw. Think of each part of your
     body until you are completely at ease.
         Now, take deep breaths, at least three or four times.
     Picture the meeting in progress, the way you are dressed,
     and the questions that might be directed to you. Imagine
     yourself confident, decisive, making a good impression,
     and feeling very good about yourself. You are relaxed
     and enjoying the meeting.
         By the time you are actually at the interview, you will
     feel so much more confident, you could end up enjoying
     it. Once I did this exercise the night before an important
     job interview. It was a position for a Distribution Center
     Manager for a Fortune 500 company. Although it wasn't
     considered a woman's field, I was lucky enough to get
     the job over the 14 male finalists. I really believe going
     through the imagery had a lot to do with my success.

This also works for public speaking or any new encounter. Of course, for this to work properly, you must also be thoroughly prepared.

2. If you have been putting off an unpleasant task, such as cleaning a closet, washing the car, writing a letter, or repairing an appliance, imagine how it would be if it were done. Picture how great it looks, the feeling of accomplishment, what a good job you did. It didn't really take so long to finish; it was just a matter of getting started.

3. This same exercise can be applied to anything you would like to accomplish, like finding a better job, inventing a better mouse trap, asking for a raise, writing a book, taking up a new sport, saving money, dieting, winning new friends, or even improving your health.

4. When you have a headache or other annoying ache or pain, imagine how it would feel if the pain and discomfort were gone. Try pushing it away. If it is a headache, picture an imaginary spout on top of your head. See all the pain and pressure, in the form of steam, being released through this imaginary spout.

    When any part of your body isn't functioning properly, imagine that part working perfectly. This is certainly no substitute for seeing your physican, but it can help, along with medical care.

5. Have you taken up a new sport, or would you like to improve an existing one? Sit in a chair, or lie down. Take deep breaths, and slowly relax each part of your body from head to toe.

    Now picture the environment where the sport takes place. Let's use golf as an example. Smell the newly mown grass. Feel the sod under your feet as you address the ball with correct stance and follow through. Strike the ball perfectly, and watch it soar through the air as it nears the next hole. Practice chipping onto the green, and finally do your putting. Do all this imagining as if you are really "there", as if it is truly happening. Strange as it may seem, if you do this fifteen or twenty minutes each day, it will improve your game. Another example of the power of the mind.

Imagery also works for relationships. First visualize a person acting the way he should or the way you would like him to act. You will condition yourself to treat this person in a manner consistent with the new image. You can wipe away your negative feelings and resentments. Now he will be more conducive to acting as you would like him to.

Gain Peace of Mind and Security
Never "sell your soul to the company store." In other words, don't give up your freedom to decide where you would like to work and what type of work you would like to do, simply because of a financial bind. Listed below are a few suggestions to help you be independent and reduce financial worries.

1. Make your credit cards your friends. Do not let the cards control you. Do not get to the point where you are cutting up your plastic because you spend too much. Charge only what you can pay for in one month. Think of the cards as cash: How much money do I have to work with this month? This will eliminate very high finance charges. It doesn't take much for these accounts to get out of hand. Keep them from becoming a burden.

2. Pay yourself first. Save something each month, and watch your investment grow. Increase the amount you

save as your income grows. Soon you will be taking pride in your nest egg and will actually hate to dig into it.

3. Learn all you can about where your money will earn the most interest and also be safe. Many stock brokers give free seminars; attend one. The library offers many books on investing, and some good ones are targeted for the lay person.

4. As soon as you have more money in a savings account, you will be able to get better interest on your checking account. Some brokerage houses offer much better rates than banks and still allow you to have risk free investments.

5. When your monthly bills come in, make out the checks and have them ready to mail, but do not put stamps on them. Note the day the bill is due. Plan on mailing them five days before the due date. (Earlier if it takes longer than five days to reach the destination). Write this date on the envelope, where the stamp will be placed. Keep a basket or box on your desk, or bookcase, to hold these bills and your stamps. Check the dates often and make sure you stamp them, and mail them on time. This process will allow you to leave your money in the checking account earning interest for a longer period of time. The interest does add up.

6. Consult a financial planner. If you don't know a good one, contact a business editor at a large newspaper. He or she may be able to give you a list of experts in your area. Talk to several planners before you decide which one fits your personality. Some of these people charge a fee to do plans, others sell products and get a commission, and still others do both. If your situation is

simple, the fee should be small. Any good financial
planner should be willing to have at least a half hour get-
acquainted meeting without any charge. At the meeting,
ask about credentials, references, and make sure you
fully understand the services and fees. Just remember,
getting money is hard, keeping it is even harder.

7. Don't be influenced by commercials and ads. Just
   because you own a VCR or some sleek new car is no
   guarantee that you will be happy. Worrying about how to
   make all the payments takes the joy out of ownership.

8. Forget about keeping up with the Jones'. Who are they
   anyway? A family invented by the Madison Avenue
   hucksters? If your friends are only impressed by your
   possessions, are they really friends? If you want to be
   poor, live like you are rich!

9. Don't buy things because you are bored. Spending
   money will not make you less bored. When you get the
   urge to splurge, instead do something that is free. Go to
   the library (you can study finance), art gallery, or museum.
   Volunteer some time to your local hospital, nursing
   home, or childrens' home. Take a walk, clean a closet, or
   wash the car. Plan your next vacation, or make a budget
   and stick to it.

10. When you do make purchases, try to do the following:

    a) Once you have decided a specific item is really what
       you want, give yourself enough time to see what the
       market place has to offer. Do not buy impulsively.

    b) Try to buy on sale, whether it be a major purchase or a
       ten dollar item. Don't be afraid to ask when it will be
       reduced.

c) Forget designer goods, but always purchase quality merchandise. Do you really want to pay more to advertise some merchant's name? That is really what you are doing.

11. When you purchase homeowners insurance, always insist on "replacement value." By doing this, if you have a claim, you will receive whatever it costs to replace your loss (minus the deductible) instead of what the item was worth when purchased. This also applies to renter and condominium insurance.

12. When you purchase condominium homeowners insurance, ask for "assessment loss" on the policy. If you should be assessed for a liability suit, or major project, your insurance might cover it.

13. Throughout the year, keep a tax folder in an easy access area. Each time you have a tax related purchase or expenditure, such as a visit to a physican or dentist, pay your property tax, buy a medical appliance or have a prescription filled, put the receipt in your folder. This will save you many hours of hunting and sorting at tax time. It will also help you to take full advantage of any possible deductions.

Do Your Commercial Reading In Comfort
Many things arrive in the mail that you would like to go over more thoroughly, but there never seems to be enough time. You either store them with intentions of getting to them or toss them upon arrival. Here is an alternative. Keep all those interesting catalogs and sales pitches next to your favorite TV chair. When a commercial comes on, you can do your own commercial reading.

Grayce

The last time I saw my maternal grandmother I was only seven, but I still remember her snappy black eyes; they were electrifying. I couldn't imagine anyone not doing what she asked. Her bobbed hair was wavy and as dark as her eyes. There was no gray, in spite of her fifty-odd years. Grayce was very slim and only 5'-2". She always moved quickly and did everything fast, as if she had a schedule to meet. She was a very fiesty lady. There is a story about her that I adore, so I will share it with you.

Grayce was about 30 when she was left with 9 stair-step children to raise by herself. This happened around 1910.

She had a small flat above a store in Olympia, Washington. It wasn't very big, but they made the best of it. To support her family, she did sewing during the day and made coffee and donuts for the nightly poker parties. These get-togethers were held in a large room behind the barber shop and attended by many of the local citizens.

One day when she was called away to do a fitting for a prominent citizen whom she hoped to get as a client, she had to leave the two youngest children at home alone. My Mother Violet was 4, and her sister Gladys was 5. The older children would be home from school very soon, so the girls would not be there alone very long.

As soon as Grayce left, Violet went out on the balcony, where she was forbidden to go. Somehow, she lost her little shoe through the grating, and it fell to the sidewalk.

While Violet and Gladys were still worrying about getting the shoe back before their Mother

returned, there was a a knock at the door. Gladys
opened it, to find a very tall man holding the
missing slipper. He introduced himself as Al
Robbins. The girls were so delighted to see that
their problem had been solved that they invited the
stranger in. Acting very grown up, Gladys asked if
he would like some tea. He declined, because of an
appointment, but promised to return. Al asked that
the visit be their little secret and bid the girls
goodbye. Still thinking of Violet being on the
forbidden balcony, the girls were eager to agree.

Al returned often with fresh eggs, milk, meat,
and other much needed groceries. He brought toys,
and special treats. All the children looked forward
to his visits. He always came when Grayce was
away. She was very grateful for all the help, but
couldn't figure out who the Good Samaritan was.

One night at the poker party, while Grayce was
serving her usual coffee and donuts, Al stood up
and stretched. It was the end of the hand, but still
early, as he said, "Well, I have to check on my
kids."

Grayce stared in disbelief, because the whole
town knew that Al had no children of his own. In
fact, he was the town's most eligible bachelor. Now
she knew who had befriended her family.

It wasn't long until they were married. Al's
family was so disgruntled over his marrying a
women with all those children that they disin-
herited him. Al had loved Grayce from afar for so
long that being with her and the children was more
important than money he hadn't earned.

They boarded all the children out and went to
Alaska to make their fortune. While Al searched for
gold, Grayce made beautiful dresses for the "ladies

of the night." These women were very generous,
and when they ordered luxurious silks and satins,
they always included enough material for frocks for
each of Grayce's five daughters.

After a year in the North, they returned to
Olympia where they gathered their family together
and bought a farm. They had a son and called him
Alta. Al was a good father and husband to them
all.

Do Your Baby A Favor

First Baby

The nurse stopped at my bedside, clip board in hand. My beautiful, healthy baby was two days old, and I was on "cloud nine." This was my first experience in a military hospital. There were no frills, but the important things were taken care of.

"Mrs. Gill, would you sign this release? It's just routine." Said the nurse crisply.

"What is it for?" I asked. "We need your signature before we can circumsize your baby," she responded. "That won't be necessary," I replied.

The nurse frowned. "It would be a good idea if you would reconsider."

"Thank you for your concern, but I don't want this procedure done."

"Have you thought about hygiene?"

"I don't think that is an issue."

"What if your son wants this done when he is an adult? It is much easier and less painful to do now."

I couldn't contain myself any longer. Feeling I had given her enough of a bad time, I smiled and retorted, "There is only one problem, you see, I have a baby girl!"

Plan Ahead

The most precious gift you can give your baby is good health. One way this can be accomplished is for *both* parents to be in optimum health at least six months prior to conception.

There is an organization in England called FORESIGHT that has been helping prospective parents do just that for the last eight years. Many couples who have had children with birth defects or who were unable to conceive are now having healthy offspring with the help and education of FORESIGHT.

Now a non-profit organization in California called Pre-Conceptual Care, Inc. is doing the same thing for U.S. couples. No matter where you live, they can advise you.

If you are able to visit personally, some of the things included are: lab tests, examinations, and dietary controls. Life style, eating habits, and contraception are discussed at length. Pre-Conceptual Care helps the future parents have babies free of allergies, learning problems, infections, and especially serious birth defects. This is done by *both* parents taking responsibility for being in the best health and learning about the effects of what they put into their bodies has on the fetus.

For further information call or write:

Pre-Conceptual Care, Inc.
P.O. Box 2436
Castro Valley, California 94546
(415) 582-0183

Give Your Baby Nutritious Foods

Don't give your baby canned, processed foods when there are so many fresh, nutritious foods you can use to help him grow strong and healthy. Canned foods lose much of their value in processing and storage. Wouldn't you rather know exactly what you are feeding your baby?

If you nurse your baby, he will get all the necessary

nutrients, if you eat properly. He will not only be more satisfied and sleep better, but will be protected from childhood diseases because of your immunities.

A friend decided not to nurse her baby and he contacted Chicken Pox at age two months, which is very unusual. Perhaps it could have been prevented if she had nursed him.

Do not smoke during the period you nurse your baby. It has been found that nicotine shows up in a mother's milk as little as 1/2 hour after she had smoked a cigarette. Babies should not be subjected to nicotine in their diet, or in their environment for that matter. What better motovation could *both* parents have to quit smoking then the protection of their precious child from harmful chemicals?

My daughter-in-law nursed Sierra until she returned to her job. Sierra was then put on one of those chemically manufactured formulas. By the time she was seven weeks old, she was demanding eight ounces of milk every three hours or less. She had a tremendous amount of gas, and her stools were liquid and yellow.

By her ninth week, the doctor changed the formula to another synthetic brand. Now she was eating seven times a day. In her short life she had had a viral infection and a bad chest cold. The doctor also felt she weighed too much.

Sierra's parents finally took her to a nutritionist when she was ten weeks old. He was able to solve her problems with a formula that filled all of Sierra's nutritional needs.

She was very satisfied. No more gas or diarrhea. This formula provided all the nutrients she would need until she started eating food. The good bacteria in the acidophilus made her bowel movements normal by creating a friendly flora.

This formula improved her own lymphatic capability, so that she was able to fight off infection. She began thriving. Sierra was slim, yet firm and growing. No more excess body fluid, which looked like healthy body fat, but was not.

This formula, along with oils also provided calcium for bone growth, all the needed minerals, B complex, sugars, vitamins A, D, and E along with fatty acids.

The basis of the formula was goats milk, which is the most like mother's milk, and easy to digest with no high phlegm reaction.

The synthetic formulas that were first used for Sierra, had a soya base, which is an incomplete protein and was also loaded with unnatural chemicals. Following is the formula and oils recommended by the nutritionist:

Formula
- 6 to 8 oz. bottle goat's milk, either fresh or dry.
  (If dry is used, follow directions on can.)

- 1/2 teaspoon unsulphered blackstrap molasses. (DO NOT INCREASE THIS AMOUNT babies get an abundance of iron in their liver, passed on from their mothers.)

- 1 tablespoon liquid acidophilus (keep refrigerated).

- 1 small pinch kelp powder.

- 1/4 teaspoon brewers yeast powder.

- 1 teaspoon Solgar Liquid Pediatric Vitamins.

Oils
- 5 drops (or 1/2 teaspoon) Viobin Wheat Germ Oil. Drop directly into infant's mouth at morning feeding. Keep refrigerated.

•   5 drops (or 1/2 teaspoon) Hain Cod Liver Oil.
Drop directly into infant's mouth at afternoon
feeding. Keep refrigerated.

Always check with your baby's doctor before making any
changes in his or her diet.

My pediatrician broadened my babies' food variety as
they started getting teeth, and I gave them steamed vegetables
that I mashed. This included vegetables like carrots, peas,
spinach, green beans, and potatoes. They really enjoyed
apple that I scaped with the side of a spoon. (Peel the apple
and scrape the fruit, it is like uncooked applesause). Other
favorites were melon, orange, pear and mashed banana with
egg yolk. I gave them ground chicken, liver, and fish that I had
prepared for the rest of the family.

Do not give your baby solid foods before age six months,
unless you have the approval of your doctor. It is believed that
children have a better chance of being allergy-free if they do
not have solid foods before this age. It will be easier to follow
this rule if you nurse your baby.

Tips For Sleeping Through The Night
Getting up in the night to feed a crying infant can be a
frustrating and tiring problem for the entire family. This is
particularly true if it continues over a long period. It can also
spoil the parent-child bonding, play havoc with the parents'
relationship, make it difficult to cope at work or at home, and
in extreme cases cause child abuse. Listed below are some
suggestions to encourage your baby to sleep through the
night.

1.   After a baby is two months old or over 11 pounds, you
can start the process of training him to sleep all night.
Before this time, a baby usually needs two nightly
feedings, but never wake him to eat unless your doctor

has advised it. Just remember, the more he eats during the day, the more he will want to eat at night.

2.   The longer you stretch out the daytime feedings, the longer the baby will be able to sleep at night. Hold him more during the day, and use a pacifier if it is necessary. Aim toward feeding your baby only every four hours and only four times a day by age four months. By six months, you should be able to cut down to only three feedings a day, with light nutritious snacks in between.

3.   When baby wakes in the night hungry, cut down on the amount of milk you give him by one ounce, and limit the nursing time to twenty minutes. This can be done whether the baby is bottle or breast fed.

4.   Don't let the baby associate drinking milk with falling asleep. At the evening feeding, hold him. Do not allow him to have this bottle in his crib. Put the baby to bed awake when he is satisfied, and he will learn to go sleep without a bottle. You can use the pacifier if he needs extra sucking.

5.   At three months, when he wakes up in the night, let him cry for five or ten minutes before you go to him. Do not turn on the light, change his diaper, or pick him up. Pat him and tell him goodnight and then leave him. If he continues to cry, check him every fifteen or twenty minutes, but don't stay more than a minute. He may cry for over an hour at first, but soon he will be sleeping all night.
     If you suspect a physical reason for your baby's night crying, be sure to check with the doctor.

Control Baby's Environment
    My Mother always told me to dress my infant the same as I

would myself if I were inactive. New mothers have a tendency to keep their babies too warm and the room temperature too high. Feel the top of your baby's head. If it is moist, then he is too warm. It's better to have the room a little on the cool side. He can then build up his resistance. Make sure he is properly covered.

To prevent cold air and drafts from reaching your infant's crib, place newspapers under the mattress (on top of the springs). Do not have the crib on an outside wall. If you must use an outside wall, cover the wall with cardboard or plywood. Use bumper pads around the crib to protect the baby from crib rails and also to keep out drafts.

If your baby is congested, he will sleep more comfortably if you place a small folded blanket under the mattress (beneath where his head and shoulders will rest). This will elevate his head so that he can breathe more freely. The blanket will stay in place better under the mattress than directly beneath the child.

Use the same weight clothing throughout a season. As an example, in the winter make sure your child's sleepers and undershirts are all the same weight. Switching from one weight to another can cause colds.

If you can't keep a window open at night, air the room out during the day. Be sure your child is never in a draft. When you take your new infant outdoors, be sure his head is covered and no wind can reach his face. Swallowing cold air can cause colic.

Don't expose him to bright sunlight. His eyes are very sensitive. A protective bonnet is a good solution. Ears should not be exposed to wind or cold air.

It won't be long until your baby is big enough to get into everything. Start early to child-proof your home. Lock up guns, medications, chemicals, and any other dangerous substances. Attach accordian gates to the kitchen door and all stairwells. Baby can watch you cooking without the chance of being burned or getting under foot. Never back the car out of the driveway until you know exactly where your child is.

Keep Your Baby Comfortable

1. Sleeping positions are important. If your new baby can hold up his head, and his bed or bassinette has a firm mattress, put him on his tummy. This is most important after feeding. **Be sure he can turn his head from side-to-side**. Do not leave him on his tummy for periods longer than 20 or 30 minutes. This position puts pressure on his back and flays out his feet. Never leave the new baby on his back. It could cause him to choke if he spits up. Sleeping on his back could also cause the back of his head to be flat.

   Change his position often, and place him on his side most of the time. Put a blanket (as a wedge) behind him to keep him from rolling over. When you rotate sides, turn him around so he is always able to look out into the room. This is only necessary if the crib is against a wall.

2. Be sure the blanket is not too tight or heavy over his sensitive feet and toes.

   When you lay him down, be sure his little undershirt or kimono is pulled down smoothly so he is not lying on a fold of material. If your hair is long, keep it out of his face. He can't tell you when he is uncomfortable.

3. Place a flannel diaper over the area where his head rests. Tuck it in and make a smooth, firm surface. If he drools, spits up, or sheds his first hair, it is easier to change the diaper instead of the whole sheet or receiving blanket. Even if you plan to use disposable diapers, a dozen flannel or gauze diapers will come in very handy.

4. Speaking of diapers, receiving blankets make very good night diapers for older babies and toddlers. Fold the blanket "kite" shaped, and line with a diaper folded rectangularly. Cover with plastic pants, or for older children, a piece of plastic can be pinned directly to the diaper.

5. Dress your baby comfortably. See that clothing is large enough not to bind. If there is any elastic on the waist, wrists, or ankles, be sure it is loose enough so that it won't leave a mark. Make sure all material that touches baby is soft, including ruffles, collars, and lables. Remember, he can't tell you when something pinches or scratches.

6. If cutting your baby's fingernails is a traumatic experience, do the cutting while baby is relaxed and asleep.

7. Be sure to give your baby plenty of water to drink. When he awakens, he will probably be thirsty. Of course, a new baby will be famished upon awakening, so give him his milk. Provide water between feedings. That is how my babies learned to drink from a cup. When they were three months old, I started giving them sips of water.

8. Keep baking soda on hand. If your baby spits up, the dry baking soda rubbed on the area will eliminate the sour smell. This is very effective when you are away from home. Keep a little dry soda in your diaper bag.

   I also kept baking soda in a large salt shaker and used it if my babies even showed the slightest sign of diaper rash. I sprinkled it on them after washing their bottoms with a warm, wet cloth.

See That Toys Are Safe
Toys should encourage a child to play, to imagine, and to

create. Things like blocks or miniature life objects are toys
that teach. If a toy is battery operated and plays *for* the child
(like a bear blowing a horn) than it is not a real learning tool.
Listed below are some of our favorites:

1. A washcloth fascinated my babies when they were a
    couple of months old. They would hold it up, turn it
    around, and put it in their mouth. They seemed to like
    the texture of the material.

2. They especially liked small, inflated soft plastic animals.
    They were light weight, brightly colored, and easy to
    handle. They could be used in the tub when they were
    older. These little giraffes, bears, and horses were good
    for teething as well.

3. The little plastic telephones were always a favorite.
    They played with them for years, and the phones were
    pretty indestructable. Cutting off the cord to separate
    the receiver from the phone is a good safety measure.

4. When my children were small and still putting every-
    thing in their mouths, I always washed their toys in warm
    soapy water before they handled them.

5. As they became toddlers, they loved to get into the lower
    kitchen cabinets, so I had one that contained only things
    that wouldn't hurt them. In this storage area were lids,
    plastic utensils, strainers, and measuring cups. They
    soon learned that this cabinet was theirs, and filled with
    many treasures.

6. Especially after the Christmas holidays there are so
    many new toys. Hide a few for a restless day. Rotate toys
    often. Do not give them so many play things that they get

confused. This does not include a favorite toy that they always want with them.

7.   For children that are a little older, a trip to the lumber yard will provide toys that will give many pleasant hours of constructive play. Large string bags of smooth wood ends make wonderful blocks. If the children are old enough, a hammer and nails add more creativity to the fun.

8.   Large cartons, such as toilet tissue, or appliance boxes, are fun for older children. They can be used for "camps," or for rolling around the yard, or flattened; for sliding down grassy hills. What a good way to get rid of excess energy! These cartons make good temporary play pens for visitors, when you are beyond the play pen stage.

9.   All toys should be safe. Examine them to see that there is nothing to hurt your baby or child. No sharp edges, no parts that can become detached, and no unsafe colors. These are just a few of the things to watch for.

Bath Time

Young children usually love to play in the bathtub, especially if they have water toys. To keep all the plastic toys together, place them in a net onion sack. Place the sack full of toys over the faucet handle to drain and store when bathtime is over.

Be sure your child is not left unattended in the tub. It only takes a few moments for a child to slip below the surface of the water, lose control and panic, or become frightened and unable to sit up. Do not leave your baby for a moment. Do not run to answer the phone; let it ring or bring it with you if it has a long cord. Do not respond to someone knocking at the door unless you first take your child out of the tub.

Speaking of bathtime, I used this period to teach my babies to feel comfortable in the water and prepare them for learning to swim. I would wring out a washcloth over their heads, using only a small amount of water at first, and then increasing the amount. Then, as they became used to water on their faces, I would dip their faces into the water. This way they learned to hold their breath. When it came time for swimming lessons, they learned to swim very quickly.

Do Your Children A Favor

Popcorn And Christmas Trees

Summer was almost over,and it was time for the ritual of buying school clothes for Susan's first grade year. A specialty shop was having a sale on camel hair coats, so off we all went to the shopping center. While Susan tried on coats, Steven 4-½ and Jeff 3-½ held 16 month old Kevin's hands as they stood nearby.

Across the room, popcorn started pouring forth from the vending machine. The boys asked if they could get some. I told them yes. It seemed like a good diversion, and I turned my attention back to the project at hand.

Suddenly a sales clerk screamed and ran to unplug the popcorn machine. Jeff was crying when I ran to him. His arm was stuck in the mouth of the vending machine. He had tried to get more popcorn when the machine stopped. We couldn't tell what was holding his finger, hand, or arm, and no one had a Phillips screw driver to disconnect the front panel.

Jeff had calmed down, but we were all pretty frantic by the time the police, fire department, and a doctor arrived. The hero, a man with the proper screw driver, finally freed him. Jeff's thumb was slightly flattened from the pressure of his 45 minute imprisonment. We made a quick trip to the hospital, followed by a TV crew. After the doctor released Jeff, the reporters begin asking him questions, but he was so embarrassed he simply hung his head.

We were all embarrassed, and Susan never did get her camel coat. The store sent a representative to our home, and we reluctantly accepted $100.

The first year we were alone (after the divorce), we had all kinds of minor catastrophes - adjusting to our new life style.

At Christmas time that year, we were in a Sears Catalog Office. While I looked for presents in the big book, Jeff asked if he could get into the little pedal car under the Christmas tree. The manager overheard him and said, "Of course you may, that's what it's there for." What he did not know was that the tree lights were wrapped around the car wheel! As Jeff started pedalling, the large tree came tumbling down leaving a trail of tinsel and broken bulbs.

The manager was very understanding, but I'm sure he was glad to see us leave. I did the shopping by phone.

The Little Match Maker

It was early September, and the three older children had started back to school. Four year old Kevin and I decided to spend the Indian Summer morning at the beach. I was sunbathing and reading, enjoying playing hookey from my domestic routine. His sand pail and shovel forgotten, Kevin was busy watching a man sawing fence posts from driftwood logs. The man patiently answered Kevin's many questions about the saw and the posts. They spent a couple of hours together until we were ready to leave. They both came over to the blanket and the man said, "He's a charming little boy and I enjoyed his company."

The next morning when the phone rang, I was surprised to learn that it was the man from the beach. He had called to invite Kevin and me to lunch. Ignoring his invitation, I asked,

"How in the world did you get our phone number?"

"You live in a white house with green trim. You don't have a Daddy anymore, and you just love to go to dinner and dancing."

Children are a responsiblity, but also a blessing. The more diligent your effort, the greater your reward. Don't expect to be a good parent by instinct. Learn all you can by reading, observing other parents, taking classes, and, if necessary, getting professional help.

SERVE your children. Give them **LUCK**. Help them **CHARGE** into the world.

By **SERVE**, I don't mean to do things for them or give them things. I mean to provide them with:

> Stability
> Education
> Responsibility
> Values
> Example

By **LUCK**, I don't mean to give them a rabbit's foot and hope for the best. I mean give them and teach them:

> Love
> Understanding
> Consideration
> Kindness

By **CHARGE**, I don't mean to blindly "tilt windmills." I mean to help them understand the need for and how to develop:

> Cheerfulness
> Health
> Ability
> Rules
> Goals
> Experience

Let's examine the above in some detail.

SERVE

1. Stability
       Children need a "safe haven." A secure environment
    that they know and understand, a retreat where they will
    be understood. A place where they are supported and
    assisted in preparing for their next venture into this big
    world.
       This includes a family and a home. Hopefully, two
    parents, one male and one female, with love, under-
    standing, and wisdom, and who present *one united front*
    to their family. In today's society, this is not always
    possible, and sometimes a single parent family is better
    than conflict in an unstable environment.

2. Education
       Life is a continual learning process. When we cease
    to learn, we cease to progress. You have almost complete
    control (and responsibility) over your children during
    their first years when they have the greatest potential for
    learning.
       Teach them all that you know. This includes arts,
    crafts, skills, and practical knowledge as well as academic
    knowledge.
       Teach them to be inquisitive, alert to their surround-
    ings, and how to learn. Allow them to try new things, and
    praise their achievements. They will try even harder and
    do better next time.
       Expose them to good books and music and give them
    creative materials. Start when they are very young. They
    are usually capable of much more than we can imagine.
    Answer all their questions. There are so many things
    they want to know, so many wonders to explore.

3. Responsiblity
       Allow them the "privilege" of being a responsible

member of the family. Even toddlers can help by picking
up their own toys and waiting on themselves. As they
grow older, increase their share of caring for their home.
If everyone does his or her share, it prepares them for
caring for themselves and cooperating with others and
leaves more time for shared family fun and activities.

4.   Values
        Try very hard to keep your promises. Let your
children know they can depend on you. Admit to them
when you make a mistake.
        Try to get them to follow through on anything they
start. This will help them to think through what they
really want to begin the next time.
        Teach them the importance of going to school *every*
day. This also applies to anything they are committed to
like sports, jobs, or meetings.
        Make them aware of community service. Help them
to feel compassion for less fortunate people by helping
to improve the community in some way.
        Teach them to share what they have with their
siblings and friends.
        By example, show them how to express compassion,
to help and to be friends to those less fortunate or
handicapped.

5.   Example
        Most everything suggested above can best be taught
by example.

LUCK

1.   Love
        Give your children all the love you can. However, this
does not mean spoiling them. If you really love them,

prepare them for the future. They are not your alter-ego; they are real people who need all the help they can get to grow up and lead productive lives. Love them with open arms; do not smother them. Show your love by preparing them for life. Being totally responsible for another human being can be the biggest and most important contribution you make to humanity.

2.   Understanding
       Really listen to what they say. Have compassion and put yourself in your children's shoes. Try to make objective decisions. Be close to them so they will talk openly to you. Know where they are, what they are doing, and whom they are with.

3.   Consideration
       Teach your children to be thoughtful of others. Good manners mean a lot more than social niceties. Manners help teach consideration of others while forming good habits. If you are considerate of your children, and treat them like you would treat an adult, they will learn by example to be considerate of others.

4.   Kindness
       If children are treated with kindness and compassion, they will be more likely to respond that way to others. When they are very young, see that they do not mistreat toys and stuffed animals. This will be a beginning so that they treat people kindly later.

CHARGE

1.   Cheerfulness
       Smile. Try not to take out your moods on your children. Enjoy them. Have fun with them; they grow up

so fast. Before you know it, they will be out on their
own.

2.   Health
      The greatest gift you can bestow on your children is
good health and good health habits. Start teaching them
early about good nutrition. Keep them clean, and they
will want to be clean. Keep their home clean and orderly,
and, hopefully, that is the way they will want to help keep
it. See that they get regular medical and dental check-
ups. Don't make them afraid of these visits by saying
"poor baby." Let them know that these professionals are
there to help keep them well. Teach them the importance
of good nutrition and how it will affect their future
performance and health. Be observant. Make sure their
eyesight and hearing are up to par. Are they walking,
running, and sitting in a normal manner?

3.   Ability
      Never underestimate children's abilities. Expect a
lot from them, and always praise their efforts and ac-
complishments. If they show a special interest, talent, or
flair for anything worthwhile, encourage them to develop
it.

4.   Rules
      Restrictions are a good form of reprimand. Being
grounded for a week, or not being able to attend a game,
party, or show, really has a lasting effect. If you back
down, the punishment is wasted, and you have lost
control. Be consistent in your discipline. Let the children
know what to expect.
      When siblings argue among themselves, send them
to another room. They usually want an audience.
      Talk with your children, and be a good listener.

Expect the same from them. Do not let them interrupt you when you are talking to them or someone else. Do not let them take advantage while you are on the phone.

Do nothing to hurt their self esteem. Never call them stupid, clumsy, or a poor reader. Let them know when you are displeased with their actions, but be supportive. If you have a temper, wait and discuss the problem when you have cooled down. Going for a walk first might help. Let them know that you aren't perfect, that sometimes you make the wrong choices, too.

5.   Goals

Instill in them the importance of a good education in the field of their choice, not yours. Of course, this does not mean you can not guide them to the field that will best fit their temperment and talents.

Help them set short term goals for the things they would like to do now. This will build good habits for future planning.

Encourage them to improve themselves by raising their grades, perhaps make the honor roll. To make a new friend each day if they are shy or introverted is a fine goal. Other goals could be: To excel in some sport by trying to make the first team or preparing for the Olympics; studying art and preparing for a one man show; developing a musical talent and working toward a debut.

6.   Experience

Remember that every encounter, adventure, trial, and tribulation that your child has will add up to how he will handle experiences when he is an adult. Do not over protect him from life's lessons. Do not cheat him out of these experiences.

Review this material once in a while. I hope it helps you while in the process of preparing your child for the best possible future.

Now for a couple of hints you might find useful:

If you are a single working parent and have "latch-key" aged children, I'm sure you sometimes have mixed emotions about responsibilities to your job, and to your children. You know you can't expect your boss to understand if you are always leaving for some minor crisis at home or school, and yet, you know you must do the best for your family. Here is how I solved the problem (and reduced some of the pressure and worry). I was able to stay at work instead of being absent every time one of my children had an upset stomach, or a routine dental appointment.

I found a non-working, reliable mother in our neighborhood and made a contract with her. She would bring the ailing child home. (Of course, if this was more than a minor ailment I would meet them at home.) She would also take them to any routine appointment or class. I paid her a pre-arranged fee for each incidence, although actually there were very few. She was glad for the extra income, and I was finally able to concentrate on my job knowing my children were in good hands.

Halloween in July? Next time the children complain of nothing to do on a summer day, try this: Get out all those old costumes. The neighbor children can join in the fun too. Panel curtains make interesting costumes. Add some old hats, and for the girls, some handbags.

Do Your Home A Favor

Auto Hints

A good **corrosion preventive for your battery** is to cover the cable terminals with vasoline. If they are already corroded, remove the terminals from their posts and thoroughly clean with a solution of baking soda and water. WIPE ABSOLUTELY DRY BEFORE RECONNECTING.

Baking soda quickly removes **splatters and road grime** from windshields, headlights, chrome, and paint. Wipe with soda sprinkled on a damp sponge or cloth and rinse.

Make **parking** your car easier with this bit of advice: If there is a glass store front where you park, use the reflection of the car to see how close you are to the auto behind you as you back in.

Have you ever missed work because your car **stalled** or would not operate? I solved this problem by making arrangements with co-workers who lived in my vicinity. We agreed to give each other a lift to the office any time we had car trouble. However, this will only work if the trouble is spotted before your neighbor leaves.

For a **clean steering wheel**, keep a box of moist towelettes in the car and clean in between car washes.

Tar and oil stains can be removed from fenders by saturating a cloth with baby oil and rubbing the area.

Another trick is to use any cola drink. Dampen a cloth with the cola and rub onto the oil and tar. This is the best thing I can think of to use cola for; it certainly beats drinking it!

When **washing** your car, use a gentle detergent and warm water. Start with the roof and work down. If the car is very dirty, hose it first. After washing and rinsing, dry with soft towels. Start with the windows, then do the chrome, and then wipe the body. By the time you get to the body, the towel will be damp, which will help remove any water spots or streaks. When waxing your car, do it in a shaded area.

If you live in an apartment or condo that allows you to wash your car on the premises, keep a hose in the trunk of your car. This makes a good storage place, and the hose is readily available.

Christmas Hints
Save **Christmas cards** you receive, and next year use them to decorate packages and to make oversized tags. (Cut out the pretty front and write on the reverse side.)

Christmas chains can be made from styrafoam bits used for packing material by most department stores. Save the white pieces and string with a needle and thread. Drape around your tree for a nice effect. Store them in small boxes after the holidays.

Make a beautiful **Christmas wall decoration** from a tree branch. Spray it white, and hang it horizontally. Add artifical birds and small ornaments.

A **Christmas Wreath** can be made easily. It can be a fun project for the whole family. You can start collecting pine cones, chestnuts, acorns, and nuts in shells throughout the year, or take an excursion to your local park or neighborhood. For the base, use a thin piece of plywood or particle board. Cut a circle the size you would like your wreath to be, and then cut out the center, so you have a donut. Now place your decorations around the board. When you are satisfied, glue them in place with rubber cement. Finish it off with a red or green velvet ribbon and you have a beautiful Christmas door wreath to greet your holiday guests.

If you would like to keep the **Spirit of Santa** alive while still teaching your children to be appreciative for all the time and money you put into giving, try this: "Santa" can fill the stockings, and you can give the expensive presents.

Cleaning Hints
Bathroom basin splashes can easily be removed by

keeping a folded washcloth at the basin. It can match the towels or the decor and will encourage family members to wipe up the counter area after each use of the basin.

Mildew between bathroom tiles can be removed with rubbing alcohol or chlorine bleach.

Clean **computer and typewriter keys** with a soft, clean paint brush. This is also effective to clean **pleated lamp shades and baskets.**

If you have a **copper drain** just below the basket in your kitchen sink, do this to make it sparkling bright: On a wet, folded cloth, pour 1 tablespoon of vinegar and ½ teaspoon of salt. Rub the area, and like magic, it will be restored to its natural copper color. You probably know that this also works on other copper, such as copper bottomed pans. Salt and vinegar is as effective as commercial cleaners and most cost effective and non-toxic.

Make a **flannel duster** by soaking an old piece of flannel in paraffin oil for several hours; wring it out, wash in tepid water, and dry. This cloth will collect dust while polishing your furniture.

Remove **fireplace chimney soot** by tossing two handfuls of table salt on a hot fire.

Protect **hearth tiles** by waxing them after they have been thoroughly cleaned with warm soapy water, rinsed, and completely dried.

Fish odors on utensils will vanish when two or three tablespoons of ammonia are added to the dish water.

Freshen **artifical flowers** by placing them in a paper bag along with a cup of corn meal and shake.

Place **oven racks** in the bathtub or wash trays, and cover with hot water and Spic & Span. Leave them overnight. All the black residue should be gone.

When **food is spilled in a hot oven**, sprinkle salt on the area. When the oven cools, brush off the burnt food, and wipe with a damp cloth.

Wipe **piano keys** with a cloth slighty dampened with denatured alcohol, and then wipe dry with a soft cloth. Never use soap on the keys, as it yellows ivory. Some marks may be removed with a soft eraser.

Remove rust from baking pans by scrubbing with a raw patato dipped in cleanser.

Scouring with automatic dishwasher detergent **prevents scratching pots and pans**.

The automatic dishwasher is a good place to clean the **range exhaust fan filter**.

Each Saturday morning, I clean all the washable surfaces in my home with Tide and Clorox (follow the manufacturer's instructions for quantity) in a bucket of hot water. This includes countertops, appliances, chairs, sliding glass door tracks, and floors - all washable surfaces. When I finish, I pour the still hot, sudsy, water into the **toilet bowl**. Besides helping to disinfect, it takes the water level down below the bowl, so that I can clean it properly with cleanser without being hindered by the water.

Make your own **window cleaner** by filling a spray bottle with three tablespoons of ammonia and one tablespoon of vinegar and fill with water.

Food Preparation

Avacados will not discolor so quickly if you leave the seed in place. This works even if it is peeled. So store the leftover avacado without removing the seed.

Beets will practically pop out of their skins after steaming if they are splashed with cold water.

One slice of bread makes ⅓ cup of dry **bread crumbs** or ¾ cup of soft crumbs.

Grate soft cheese easily by putting it in the freezer for 10 or 15 minutes before grating.

Remove chicken skin before cooking by pulling off with a cloth. Use scissors to cut off any visable fat.

Tenderize chicken or other fowl by rubbing the inside and outside with lemon juice after cleaning and before cooking.

Freshen shredded coconut by soaking in a small amount of milk for a few minutes. Drain thoroughly before using.

Separate egg whites from yolks by breaking into a funnel. The white passes through and the yolk remains.

Hard boiled egg shells can be easily removed by rinsing with cold water immediately after cooking. Wait until the water boils before placing eggs in the pan.

⅛ of a teaspoon of **garlic** powder equals one small garlic clove.

Store ice cubes in paper bags in the freezer when you are making extra ice. They will not stick together.

Marinate in a plastic bag to avoid the mess. Place a plastic bag in a bowl large enough to hold the contents to be marinated. After putting in the fowl or meat, cover with the marinade. Twist the bag securely closed and carefully turn over until the sauce is evenly distributed. Put in the refrigerator and turn twice during soaking period.

Peel onions first, and then prepare celery to prevent **hands smelling of onion**.

After shelling peas, save the **pea pods** to use for soup flavoring. Do the same with celery tops. They can be stored in the freezer until needed.

More **poultry dressing than bird?** Place the stuffing in an oiled baking dish. Place the neck, giblets, or gizzards on top and cover. Bake along with the fowl. It will give the extra dressing a nice flavor, even though it is not cooked inside the bird.

Rice grains will stay separate if a teaspoon of lemon juice is added to each quart of cooking water.

A little oatmeal adds much flavor and richness when used as a **soup thickener**.

Jewelry

If your **beads need re-stringing**, use dental floss; it is usually stronger than the original string.

To brighten rhinestone jewelry, soak it in gasoline for about 15 minutes, and then rub with a flannel cloth. ALWAYS USE CAUTION WITH GASOLINE BY KEEPING AWAY FROM OPEN FLAME, AND USE ONLY IN A WELL VENTILATED AREA, PREFERABLY OUTDOORS.

Toothpaste is another good **jewelry polisher** and safer to use.

Laundry

If you do your laundry in a public laundromat, carrying all the clothes is quite enough. Leave your cumbersome detergent and bleach boxes or bottles at home. Instead, lay a soiled hand towel flat for each load of wash you plan to do. Pour the measured amount of detergent and dry bleach into each towel. Fold them up securely, and put them with your laundry. If you use liquid bleach on your white clothes, pour it in a plastic jar that has a secure lid.

When you finish washing, separate the delicate, synthetic, and shrinkable clothes. Put them in the dryer on warm for only 3 or 4 minutes. This will partially dry them and remove any wrinkles. Finish drying them at home. Your clothes will last longer, and you will save money at the laundromat. Now put your regular clothes in this same dryer. Follow this rule at home also.

Shrunken woolens can sometimes be restored to their original shape by rinsing in soapy water instead of clear water. Soap softens wool.

Miscellaneous

75% of the cost of using your **automatic dishwasher** is in the drying. When the machine reaches the drying cycle, shut it off and prop the door open with a cloth. Let the dishes air dry.

You should notice a nice reduction in your next electric bill if you use the dishwasher very much.

Cracks in China can be removed by simmering in milk for 40 minutes. The black line will disappear and the piece of china will be stronger.

Chill candles in the refrigerator for several hours before lighting them, and they will burn much longer.

Hair on arms and legs can be bleached easily by using two parts bleaching peroxide (20 volume) and one part Ammonia. Add a small amount of either detergent or lotion to give it substance. Mix in a plastic bottle. Apply to the areas to be bleached and leave on until you see it is working. It will take from 15 minutes to one hour. If you do this in the sun it will work much faster. Rinse thoroughly when you are finished, and rub in a moisture-rich lotion. If your skin should begin to itch or sting, remove the solution immediately by flushing with water. Before you begin the first time, test the solution on a small area to make sure your skin is not sensitive to it.

Kitty Litter Odors. If you have a litter box for your cat, borax reduces the odor and makes the litter mix useable longer. Add one part borax to six parts litter mix. When you throw the litter away, put it in your garbage can, and it will reduce the odor there also.

Old sheets that are no longer needed or are slightly worn can be useful around the house. I use a fitted sheet over my mattress cover so that it doesn't need laundering so often, thus extending the life of the mattress cover.

Another fitted sheet can be used to protect the inner-springs if a board is used on the bed.

Old sheets come in handy when household repairs are made. They can be used to protect floors and carpets. This is especially helpful if an outside contractor is doing the work. Sheets work well to protect surfaces when painting.

White sheets make good sun bathing blankets because they reflect more light - similar to lying near water.

Used in the garden, old sheets are great to hold weeds, leaves, or grass cuttings. If you have a covered patio, use sheets to cover lawn furniture so it is clean and ready to use when you need it.

Old sheets can also be made into pillow cases.

Both white sheets and pillow cases make good bandages. Cut into 4 x 4 squares. Sterilize by boiling, and store in a plastic sack when dry.

Either a white pillow case, or pieces of sheet, make a great Halloween "ghost" decoration. Cut off the hem of the pillowcase so that it is more flimsy. With a black felt pen, draw a face on the upper half of the case. Make a small hole at the top so that it can be hung from a hanger, and you have a Halloween mobile.

A white sheet can be used under the Christmas tree. It will catch the fallen needles and look like snow drifts. You can also add a winter scene with miniature houses, a mirror "pond," bridge, and figures, depending on how involved you want it to be.

Old white pillow cases can be used under regular cases to keep pillows clean longer.

Plastic bags can be dried more quickly by stuffing with a paper towel.

Make your own sachet powder for dresser drawers and linen closets. Mix ½ ounce of lavender flowers with ½ teaspoon of powdered cloves. Make small "pillows" by using pretty cotton remnants and trim with lace. These make nice gifts.

When scissors grab or bind, rub them with your fingers. There is enough natural oil on your hands to provide the needed lubrication without the danger of getting oil on the material or paper being cut.

Sharpen scissors by cutting a piece of sandpaper with 1 or 2 clips.

Travel soap is usually made into very thin bars unless you are stopping at the best hotels. Meld several bars by immmersing in water for a moment and then pressing together. After completing your bath or shower, store the soap in a soap dish, ashtray, or plastic bag before the maid has a chance to throw it out. Collect these little individually wrapped soap bars throughout your trip and use them when you return home. This will not only be a nice momento of your trip, but also save money.

When removing wall hangings from a white wall, use white toothpaste to **fill nail holes**. This will be a temporary solution until the wall is painted.

Wallpaper makes good shelf liners. Pick a pattern you like from discontinued or remnant rolls of paper.

Pests

If your pet wears a **flea collar**, snip the end off before placing the collar on the animal and put the end tip in your **vaccuum cleaner bag**, which is a prolific breeding ground for **fleas.**

Mice and squirrels will vacate your attic if you put out mothballs.

Keep your closets and dresser drawers free of **moths and silverfish** by placing **cedar chips** in these areas. Fill cloth bags with the wood particles, and place them in drawers or on closet shelves. Cedar also has a lovely pungent odor.

Plants & Garden

To make a **custom fitting frog** for your flower arrangements, simply criss-cross strips of plastic tape over the top of your favorite vase. You will be able to arrange your flowers nicely.

Save the water from boiled eggs. It contains minerals and makes a beneficial drink for house plants. If you have leftover water from steamed vegetables, let it cool for a nourishing plant drink. (It would be better to drink it yourself, but this is another use for vitamin-rich water).

Chimney soot makes a fine **fertilizer for the garden** and for potted plants.

To **keep flowers smelling sweetly**, place a piece of charcoal in the water. A sprig of mint will keep the water fresh and add a fragrance to your bouquet.

Soak Dahlia bulbs overnight in water before planting. You will have larger more beautiful flowers. My Mother always did this, and some of her Dahlias were over a foot in diameter.

Poinsettias will bloom again the following year if you do this: At the end of October, put the plant in a very dark closet for thirteen hours and then eleven hours in the bright light. You must do this daily until it blooms. By the Christmas holidays, it should be blooming. October or November is also a good time to transplant last year's Poinsettias.

When **repotting house plants** with soil that has been used outdoors, bake the soil in the oven for at least twenty minutes to keep plants parasite free.

When working or playing in the yard keep a clock in a convenient window. You can see **what time it is** without tracking dirt or mud in the house, or wearing your watch. This is especially good for children to be able to tell what time it is.

Repairs

Find out where a **sticky door** rubs against its frame by placing a sheet of carbon paper (carbon side up) in the problem area on the frame. Then file or sand where you see a carbon mark.

Before painting cabinets and doors, cover all hardware, with petroleum jelly. This will aid in wiping up the drips. It can also be rubbed into hands, particularly around fingernails, to make clean-up easier.

Paint cabinets, **bookcases**, and **mouldings** with heavy duty, outdoor, water based, enamel paint. This paint is much stronger and will hold up better with everyday use.

Soak **neglected paint brushes** in hot vinegar to clean and make as pliable as new.

Remove fresh, water base **paint from hands and face** with shaving cream or shampoo.

Patch plaster on painted walls by mixing spackling compound with the same color paint that was originally used.

Light scratches on wood can be removed by rubbing with the cut surface of walnut meat or Brazil nut meat.

Make scratches on **mahogany or other dark wood** invisible by dyeing them with iodine and wiping immediately.

Scratches on wooden surfaces like paneling, floors, or doors, may be covered by a wax with dye. This is available at most hardware stores, and it comes in different shades.

Shoes

Prevent blisters from new shoes by placing adhesive tape in the heel area. This is especially helpful for children.

Protect good shoes from **dirty heel marks while driving**. Use a pair of old mis-matched or holey men's socks. Cut off the tow and high top for a heel guard. Wear it over your shoes while driving, but do not forget to remove it when you arrive at your destination!

Patent leather shoes can be cleaned with a damp cloth and hand soap. Vasoline helps prevent cracking and makes the shoes look shiny.

If you run out of **shoe polish**, substitute paste floor wax; its neutral color will brighten light or dark shoes.

To prevent **slipping on new shoes**, sandpaper the soles. This is a good accident-preventive for small children.

Squeaking shoes can be silenced by piercing the soles with several small holes. The holes should be placed right behind where the ball of the foot rests.

White shoe smudges or nicks can be repaired by using

typewriter correction fluid before repolishing.

Stains & Spots

BEFORE USING ANY OF THESE SUGGESTIONS
FOR STAIN REMOVAL, FIRST TEST THE SOLUTION
ON A HIDDEN PART OF THE FABRIC OR GARMENT.

For **ballpoint pen** marks, spray polyester fabrics with
hair spray, but do not breathe the spray. Marks will usually
disappear. If this does not do the trick, and the material is
washable, rub the area with white tooth paste. Pencil marks
can sometimes be removed with an eraser or by alternate applications of ammonia and detergent.

Chewing gum that is stuck on clothes may be removed
by holding a cube of ice directly on the area. This freezes the
gum and makes it possible to pick from the material.

Grass stains are stubborn, but the best method I have
found is to soak the garment overnight in a gallon of cold
water with ½ cup of ammonia. If this should fail, apply a
solution of one part alcohol to two parts water. If the stain
persists, use chlorine or peroxide bleach. Use this method on
color-fast cotton fabric only.

Remove tarnish from pewter by rubbing with raw
cabbage leaves.

Make your own **pre-wash spray** from dishwashing detergent (like Palmolive Liquid), ammonia, and water. This
also makes a good overnight soak for grass stains, blood, or
grease.

Red wine stains on washable fabrics can usually be
removed by running them under cold water and then rubbing
with a bar of soap. The soap turns the stain a light blue, which
will come out when the fabric is laundered in the normal
way.

Salt is another method of removing wine stains. Sprinkle
on the stain, and rinse in cold water.

Rust can be removed from material by spreading the

stained area over a pan of steaming water and then applying lemon juice directly to the stain. Rinse and repeat until the rust is completely gone.

To remove **scorch marks**, alternate applications of ammonia, detergent, and water. Rinse well before repressing.

Another method that works well is to add a few drops of ammonia to one tablespoon of hydrogen peroxide. Rub the mixture into the fabric, and rinse before ironing. Use this method on color-fast cotton fabrics only.

If a garment develops a **shine from ironing** without a protective cloth, make a solution of hot vinegar and water. Rub into the cloth, and rinse well before re-ironing. Use this method on cotton fabrics only.

Skunk scent can be removed from clothing by soaking in tomato juice. Rinse thoroughly in cool water and launder in the normal manner.

Wallpaper stains and spots can be removed by rubbing vertically, with a piece of soft, stale bread.

Waterspots on **suede** can be removed by gently rubbing the area with an emery board.

Water spots on **stainless steel** appliances and sinks can be removed with rubbing alcohol.

Water spots on **velvet** can be removed by holding the garment over steam from a tea kettle for a few minutes. Shake out and hang until completely dry and then brush.

White appliances that have yellowed can be restored to their original whiteness with a solution of borax. Mix a half cup in 2 quarts of warm water, and wipe the surface of the appliance. Rinse and dry.

And just as a reminder:

BEFORE USING ANY OF THESE SUGGESTIONS FOR STAIN REMOVAL, FIRST TEST THE SOLUTION ON A HIDDEN PART OF THE GARMENT.

My Favorite Products

The following products seem to do everything the manufacturer claims they will. I have never had to look for something new to take their place.

The makers of these products have no idea I am recommending them, and I receive no compensation for doing so.

Irma Shorell, Inc.
New York, New York 10022

Until finding these face care products, I was never satisfied for very long with other products. However, I had many compliments on my healthy looking skin the very first week I started using Irma Shorell. These products were developed by a dermatologist.

The products I use consist of:

Formula For Cleansing, which is a light foamy cleanser and is used with water to gently clean the face.

Derma Braze 35 consists of a clear solution applied to a wet sponge mitt that works like an abrasive on the face. The counter-clockwise motions are used to stimulate, remove dead skin, and clean thoroughly. Pores appear to be smaller after this treatment.

The final step is Moisture 25, or 35, depending on age. It seems to work on any skin type, whether it be dry, oily, or normal. I can't tell you how wonderful my skin felt after just one application.

These products are available at better department stores and can be used by both men and women.

Feathersprings International Corp.
13100 Stone Avenue North
Seattle, Washington 98133
206-545-8585

Feathersprings are flexible foot supports. They are made

in Germany and take three to four weeks for delivery. The supports are fully guaranteed for life and can be returned for any reason within 60 days. The cost for one pair is under $120. Payments can be made in installments with no fee. These supports can help back, knee, and foot problems.

When requested, they will send a kit (at no charge) to make impressions of your feet along with a short questionaire. They do the rest.

I did not hear of Feathersprings until after spending thousands of dollars on ill-fitting orthotics (custom made foot supports) that actually made my foot problem worse. Now my feet are very comfortable, no more burning soles and no more aching toe joints.

Awapuhi (A-va-poo-he) Shampoo
John Paul Mitchell Systems
P.O. Box 10597
Beverly Hills, California 90213

This gentle shampoo (especially good if you wash your hair daily) is made with ginger and coconut oil. It makes my hair easy to manage and smells good. Awapuhi is available at beauty shops and beauty suppy stores. This product can be used by both men and women.

SeaPlasma by Focus 21
San Diego, California 92121

SeaPlasma is a relatively new product. It is a moisturizer for *hair* and *skin*. It has an ingredient, NaPCA, that attracts and holds moisture. It is a clear liquid packaged in a spray bottle. It can be used after shampoo, shower, and throughout the day. It is very refreshing. SeaPlasma is nice to use at the pool and beach, while sunbathing. However, it does not take the place of a good sun screen. SeaPlasma is available at beauty shops and beauty supply stores. There is a new male line although the original Sea Plasma can be used by men as well as women.

Peters Professional Soluble Plant Food
W.R. Grace & Company
Fogelsville, Pa. 18051

This is an outdoor plant food, but I also use it on my indoor plants and flowers. My flowers bloom longer and have more buds than in previous years. My plants are healthy and full. People are always asking how I keep my plants looking so lovely. It certainly isn't because I have a "green thumb." Peters is available at nurseries and hardware stores.

Simple Green
Sunshine Makers Inc.
P.O. Box 467 Sunset Beach, Ca. 90742

Simple Green is a very concentrated cleaner. It is non-toxic and biodegradeable. It's strong enough to clean a car engine, yet gentle enough (when diluted) to use on upholstry and carpets. I especially like it for carpet stains and white-wall tires. Spraying on frying pans gets rid of fish odors and grease.

It works best with cold water, so it's great for camping and on the boat.

It's available at Grand Auto Stores and Lucky Food Stores in California. Write to the company for a source in your area.

Kiwi Kleener
Zealandia, Inc.
Redmond, Washington 98052

This luxurious duster is one of the nicest Christmas

presents I ever received. Dusting has never been one of my favorite things to do. I remember when my Mother would "write" dirty in any area I forgot to dust properly. Now I almost enjoy dusting.

This duster is made from fine lambswool and contains natural lanolin. This combination attracts and holds dust like a magnet. Yet, it can be shaken out easily when dusting is finished. I love it for hard-to-get-at-places. It works well on baskets, louvered doors, louveliers, plants, pictures, and typewriter and computer keys. The wooden handle makes it easy to reach door casings and inside lampshades.

It makes a nice gift for anyone who has to dust.

II. REMEDIES - HELP IS ON THE WAY

Gorilla Be Gone

Many children have imaginary playmates, but a ferocious looking, full grown male gorilla was almost too much of a challenge.

I remember that lazy summer afternoon when it all started. The children and I were having our usual restful, relaxing hour under the maple tree. Reading and quiet talks had replaced the afternoon naps.

Steven looked up from his coloring book. After scrutinizing his work with satisfaction he said, "Bo Bo escaped from the zoo today." He did not sound frightened or surprised, he might have said "it rained today." But he said it, I recalled later, as though it were a fact and nothing could change it.

"Where did you hear that?" I said, half listening, as I paused from my own reading. "Jamie Johnson told me," he responded very seriously for all of his five years. Funny how they always use the first and last name of friends they see every day when they first start school.

"Well, it's probably just a silly rumor," replied his very knowing sister of seven. Just then the popcicle man's bell could be heard down the street, and Bo Bo was forgotten for the moment.

A few days later, someone had thrown a rotten apple at the back screen door. As I went out to clean it, Steven ran by on his stick horse, chasing im-

aginary cowboys and Indians. When he saw the
screen splattered with pieces of decaying apple, he
stopped and said, "See, Bo Bo was here, and he
messed on the screen door."

When I tried to explain, he wouldn't listen. I
decided it was time to plan a trip to the zoo.

The next day was just the kind of summer day
that was perfect for a picnic in the park. We toured
the zoo, and Steven saw Bo Bo. He was satisfied
that the big ape was safely secured in his cage.

That night after the children were settled in
bed, Steven began to cry. When I went to him, he
howled, "Bo Bo was in my room!" "But Steven," I
reasoned, as I sat on his bed and held him close,
"You saw Bo Bo in his cage. He's locked up tight, he
gets a shock if he even touches the glass surround-
ing his cage. And if that is not enough, there is a
guard watching over him all the time." "But he did
get out," he insisted, "and I am the only one who
can see him." Again he would not listen.

I stayed with him until he fell asleep and told
myself that this would soon pass, all that was
needed was a little patience. After all, he had been
through a lot this year. First, losing his father
through divorce. It's hard to make excuses that are
believable, even to a five year old, as to why his
father doesn't come to see him. Then, this same
year he knew he would be having surgery to correct
obstructions in both kidneys.

As the months went by, Bo Bo, the famous
Woodland Park Zoo gorilla, was firmly entrenched
in our household. He didn't "appear" every night,
but he was with us several nights each week.

Steven was in the hospital a good deal of the
time that year. The nurses said Bo Bo was a

frequent "visitor" there too. Ironically, there was a
monkey tree outside Steven's window. This, he
said, was Bo Bo's nest.

A year went by, and the surgeries were success-
fully completed, and Steven was flourishing, even
looking forward to when he was old enough for
Little League. But Bo Bo was still our "star
boarder."

One typical evening, when the children were
supposedly settled for the night, and I was tired
and glad for the quiet, Steven started crying. As his
soft cry turned to a howl, I went into the kitchen
looking for an answer. In desperation, I opened
cupboard doors, not really knowing what I was
looking for. Then I spied it. Would it work? It might.
Steven couldn't read much.

I went to his room. He uncovered his head from
the blankets, tears streaming down his flushed
cheeks. I handed him a brightly colored can,
smiled, and said, "Do you know what this is?" He
looked perplexed because I was smiling. "I have a
surprise for you, Steven," He stifled a sob, as he
examined the can. "Steven, this is just our secret.
It's called Gorilla Be Gone. All we must do is spray
it in your room each night and Bo Bo will never
come back."

And he didn't, thanks to a can of air freshener.

Acne

Although teenagers are especially susceptible to this often embarrassing skin problem, it also affects adults. Not eating properly and being under stress at home, in school, and in social situations are some of the reasons. Young people are undergoing hormonal changes and rapid growth, which also adds to the problem. Listed below are some suggestions that may help provide a clear, healthy looking complexion:

1. The first thing to do is review your eating habits. Are you skipping breakfast? Are you eating a sugary, starchy, fat-laden morning meal? Does lunch consist of candy bars and cokes or French fries and hamburgers? Do you rush off before dinner is served, eating a sandwich on the run?

    You should eat three well balanced meals each day. Be sure they include grains like brown rice, barley, yellow corn meal, and oatmeal. Vitamin A and B rich foods are very important and include the following:

    Steamed or baked carrots, sweet potatoes, squash, spinach, cauliflower, turnip greens, and chard are excellent vegetables. Fruits high in vitamin A include fresh peaches, cherries, papaya, cantaloupe, persimmon, and prunes. Organ meats, cheddar cheese, wheat germ, and yeast should also be included.

2. Substitute fish for red meat at least two or three times a week. Ocean fish and sardines are most beneficial. Each night at bedtime take one tablespoon of Norwegian emulsified cod liver oil. It is much easier to take than regular cod liver oil and leaves no after taste. This rich oil will provide you with much needed Vitamins A and D in a natural form. If you take any other Vitamins A and D, such as in a multi-vitamin, be sure you do not go over the recommended daily allowance. (Vitamin A 25,000 units

Vitamin D 400 units.) These vitamins are fat soluable and can be toxic if too much is taken. Natural fish oils are the best source, with less chance of toxitity.

3. Taking one or two tablespoons of cold pressed peanut oil, sunflower oil, or safflower oil each day will provide vitamin E. This much needed vitamin will reduce scarring, both internally and on your skin surface. Keep the oil refrigerated.

4. For a snack, eat peanut butter, raw nuts, and raw sunflower seeds. Keep the seeds and nuts in the freezer to preserve their freshness and to help prevent them from becoming rancid. Dried or fresh fruit makes a refreshing snack. Air popped corn with vegetable oil and a lttle salt is quite tasty.

5. To help handle stress take a B Complex, 50 or 75 balance. B Complex is a balanced formula of all the essential B vitamins, which if not not taken together, can cause an imbalance in the body's B vitamin requirements. The proper balance of B vitamins will aid you in coping with pressures, make you think more clearly, and help you handle everyday problems.

6. Take one tablespoon of lecithin granules each morning mixed in juice or sprinkled on cereal. Lecithin is a nutritional supplement containing fatty acids, phosphorous, choline, nitrogen, and glycerol. It helps reduce fat in the liver and arteries. Besides aiding fat metabolism, the choline enhances memory and concentration. Lecithin can be purchased in most health food stores and should be refrigerated after opening.

7. Avoid animal fat, margarine, soft drinks, white flour, and sugar.

8. Squeeze fresh oranges for a drink. It is full of Vitamin C and potassium. Drink several glasses of purifying water daily. Some of the water can be substituted by the following teas:

   Parsley tea is very cleansing, nourishing to the system, and tastes pleasant. Wash a fresh bunch of parsley in cold water. Drain, and place in a large glass bowl. Add 1½ quarts of boiling water (enough to cover the parsley). Cover, and steep until cool. Pour into jars or bottles, cover, and store in the refrigerator. Drink several cups each day. Make a new batch after 48 hours.

   Burdock Root, a very purifying herb, is available at most health food stores. Steep one teaspoon of Burdock in one cup of boiling water. Drink two cups each day. One teaspoon of honey may be added.

9. Get plenty of exercise in the fresh air. Do deep breathing exercises out-of-doors or in front of an open window.

10. Witch Hazel is soothing and refreshing to the skin. It is a gentle solution distilled from the bark of the Witch Hazel plant and has been used for many years for relief of pain and discomfort from bruises and sprains. The solution can be applied to the face after cleansing. Splash some on a cotton ball and wipe over the face. No need to dry. Witch Hazel can be purchased at most drug stores.

The above suggestions may seem like a lot of changes to make all at once. Perhaps you could start gradually. You'll have to be the one to decide how important nice skin and a healthy body are to you. Maybe your face is trying to tell you something while there is still time to change. It is said that your face is the reflection of what is going on in your body.

Allergies

Often allergies can arise from poor diet or a chemical imbalance. Eating a variety of foods, never repeating the same ones more than every three or four days, may help. One example is wheat. Many people are allergic to wheat, without even knowing it. Cutting down on bread can sometimes do more than reduce calories. Some symptoms of a wheat allergy are: diarrhea, bloating, water retention, headache, or stomach pain. Usually the very thing we are allergic to is the thing we crave. Once we start eating it, we don't want to stop. This is usually true of sugar products.

Take one tablet daily of a good B Complex (50 or 75 balance). For children, ask your pediatrician about the dosage. This will help with the stress of the allergy and help your body cope with it. Sometimes when we are short of the B vitamins, an allergy develops.

Drink Comfrey tea several times daily whenever you have an allergy attack. This purifying tea can sometimes reduce the discomfort of coughing, sneezing, and rashes.

And as stated earlier, see that your diet is as well balanced as possible. Don't forget to vary the foods you eat.

Get more vitamin C in your diet by eating citrus fruits like oranges, grapefruit and lemon. Ask your doctor about taking a vitamin C supplement. Make sure it contains bioflavinoids which help utilize the vitamin C more effectively. Bioflavinoids are made from the pulpy substance inside the citrus rind. Do not cut the pulp away when eating citrus fruits. It is a good idea to take the vitamin C in granule or capsule form to prevent it from lying in your stomach in a concentrated tablet, which could cause an irritation. The vitamin C works to build resistance to allergies and will also relieve the coughing, sneezing, stuffed up feeling, and rash that accompany some allergies. If you decide to use capsules, make sure they are in a tamper-proof container.

Arteriosclerosis Prevention

Arteriosclerosis is a disease of the arteries. When arteries become clogged with fat, they cannot do their job, and strokes and heart attacks occur. The time to prevent this from happening is NOW.

Take one tablespoon of soy lecithin granules daily. Lecithin is a good housekeeper and helps to keep your arteries free of sludge by absorbing the fat and carrying it away. Keep the lecithin in the refrigerator.

Take one tablespoon of cold pressed peanut oil before each meal. Cold pressed oil has more value because it is not processed by using heat. It contains more vitamin E. Do not be concerned about the extra calories; the oil will lessen your appetite and clean your arteries at the same time. Oil stays in your stomach longer so it makes you feel full and more satisfied for a longer period of time. Be sure to keep the oil tightly closed and in the refrigerator.

Avoid saturated fats such as butter, whole milk, cream, and fatty meats. Eat plenty of chicken and turkey (with the skin removed), fish, fresh vegetables and fruits. Drink non-fat milk.

Back Pain, Lower

If you have a minor back problem, either sporadic or chronic, here are some suggestions that can relieve your discomfort:

(It is always a good idea to discuss anything new with your doctor before starting.)

1. Strenghten your stomach muscles so they can help carry the load, improve your posture, and keep your back erect. Start very slowly doing sit-ups. Knees should be bent, lower back pressed against the floor. **Do this only if there is no pain.** Do only 5 sit-ups each day for the first week. Increase to ten sit-ups the second week. Keep

increasing the number of sit-ups by five each week as long as there is no discomfort.

After completing your sit-ups, while in this position, hug your knees to the chest. Tighten your stomach and bottom muscles. Hold to the count of ten. Repeat 3 times. Be sure that your neck is well supported by tucking a pillow into it, above the shoulders and below the head.

2. When your back hurts or feels strained, try this for relief: Lie on the floor on your back in front of a couch. Scoot your bottom as close to the couch as possible with legs on the couch seat, back flat on the floor. Tighten your stomach muscles. At the same time hold in rectal muscles as if checking a bowel movement and tilt the pelvis upward. This is called a Pelvic Tilt. You can also do this while sitting or standing. When you do this exercise while lying down, be sure your neck is well supported.

3. Do not stand for more than 20 minutes in one place. If you are standing at the grocery check-out stand, put one foot on the lower rung of the shopping cart. This relieves some of the pressure on the lower back. (You can also do the above exercise.)

When ironing, doing dishes, or working on a stand-up project, keep a small stool nearby. Put one foot on it, and change feet often.

4. Sleep on your side with neck well supported, spine straight, knees bent slightly, legs together at knees and ankles. Place a small pillow between your knees to be more comfortable. If you have broad shoulders, use a small pillow or rolled towel at the waist. When turning over, do not use your neck to rotate to the other side.

Raise up, and use your arms and body.

5. Make sure you have a bowel movement every day. This
    relieves some of the pressure and helps circulation. (See
    Constipation below.)

6. When lifting, bend your knees, and let your legs, not your
    back, do the work.

7. Rest in a knee-chest position several times a day, or
    whenever you can make the time. To do this, get on your
    knees and bend forward, arms straight out behind you.
    Try to touch your shoulders to the floor. Turn your neck
    to one side. This exercise takes the strain away from the
    back.

8. Walking and swimming are both good exercises for the
    back. If you are not a swimmer, walk through the water,
    waist or chest deep. The water temperature should not
    be cold. Stay out of wind when outdoors, and don't get
    chilled.

9. Some back pain may be caused by a calcium deficiency.
    Be sure you have an adequete amount of calcium daily.
    (See Menstral Cramps below.) Ask your doctor about
    the proper dose for you.

10. Massage the painful areas with peanut oil. (See Joint
    Pain below.)

11. Take a good B Complex, 50 or 75 balance. Back pain
    causes body stress. Stress increases your need for the B
    vitamins.

12. Wear shoes that provide good support. Do not wear high
    heels.

13. This exercise is especially helpful after periods of in-activity. Sit on the edge of the bed, feet flat on the floor, and place your right palm over your left hand. Now place the back of your right hand, still clasping your left hand, across your forehead. Very slowly, twist from side-to-side. Do this 20 or 30 times. This is very beneficial after sitting. Do this exercise when you get up in the morning and again at bedtime. It can be done any other time during the day as needed. DO NOT DO THIS EXERCISE IF YOU FEEL ANY PAIN.

14. The last and most significant suggestion is easy to do, and the results will astound you. Simply walk on your hands and *feet*. Do this in your home, when you are alone if you are embarrassed. It isn't the most graceful walk, but it takes the stress and pressure off of the back. At first you may only be able to go several steps, but soon you will be able to increase your new exercise to twenty or thirty paces. You will be using different muscles, so you may be a little sore at first.
Do this walk whenever you think of it during the day, especially after sitting. Then do it again before bed.
Within a month you should notice a big improvement.
Be sure to get an okay from your health specialist before trying any of the above.

Bed Wetting

First, have the child examined by a urologist. If there are no urological problems, then proceed with the following:

Brew a tea made from equal parts of St. John's Wort and Plantain. These herbs are available at most health food stores. Steep a teaspoon of the combined herbs in a cup of boiling water and serve a quarter cup, four times each day. (Serve no later than 5 P.M.) Honey may be added to make the tea more tasty. These herbs are noted for relaxing the child.

Have an early dinner - no later than 5 PM. Make sure no stimulating foods like coffee, tea, white flour products, or white sugar products are eaten. Carbonated soft drinks are also included in this group. No liquids should be taken with dinner or for the rest of the evening. If the child complains of being thirsty, give him a small sip of water.

One of the most common reasons for this very frustrating dysfunction is FOOD ALLERGIES. Discuss the problem with a nutritionist who can find the offending food or foods. Otherwise, bed wetting could continue until the child's pelvic area grows large enough for the bladder to hold more liquid.

Let the child know you are supportive. Don't become emotional about the wet bed. If he is old enough (7 or 8), let him change his sheets each day there is an accident. I did this with my son, and it made him feel like he was contributing something in a positive way.

Make sure he is not constipated. The pressure could affect his bladder. Does he have an emotional problem? Is he trying subconsiously to get needed attention? Is he getting proper nutrition? The bed wetting may only be a symptom.

Perhaps the child is unhappy. A divorced friend of mine let her 7 year old spend a school term with his father in another state. She thought it would be a good experience for them both to get closer together. Instead, the little boy was so unhappy that he started wetting the bed. His father made him sleep in the garage for two weeks, which only compounded the problem. This whole incident was so traumatic for him that for years he would bring up the subject of his visit to his father. He did stop wetting the bed shortly after he returned home. This is probably an extreme case, but it illulstrates how important emotional stability can be.

Bladder or Urinary Discomfort

First, see a urologist to make sure there are no urological problems. If the doctor finds nothing, then try the following:

Drink at least two cups of Burdock Root tea each day. Steep 1 teaspoon of the root for 10 minutes in boiling water, cool, and sip slowly. Never use aluminum utensils when making tea. Ingestion of aluminum could happen because of a chemical reaction. Burdock Root is very cleansing and can be purchased at most health food stores.

Once a friend had a very stubborn urinary track infection after having her urinary tract dialated. The infection had not cleared up with medication. I had read about Burdock Root and told her about it. She didn't really expect it to work. After she drank two cups each day for two days, her infection was completely gone.

Burns, Minor

Run cold water over the burned area for one minute, or place a cold cloth on it if it is more convenient. Cover the area with a cloth soaked in vinegar. Relief should be noticed within 15 minutes. Serious burns should be treated by a physican.

Vitamin E can be a great help in healing burns. Puncture an E capsule with a sterile needle, and squeeze drops on the burned area. This will not only speed up healing but will also relieve the itching and soreness. There will be less chance of scarring if the vitamin E is used consistently during the healing process.

Cellulite

This "cottage cheese" effect under the skin seems mostly to be a woman's woe. Listed below are some suggestions to prevent it from occuring or help rid existing cellulite:

1.   Do not wear tight fitting clothing. Make sure waistbands, and crouches of pants are comfortable. This means they should not leave marks on your body. Check this out when you undress. Bras should fit properly and not bind. Good circulation is very important.

2.   Drink plenty of fluids but not with meals. Try to drink
      several glasses of water daily. Purifying herbal teas such
      as Comfrey and Burdock Root are very helpful. Have
      one or two cups each day instead of coffee or your
      regular tea. These herbal teas are available at most
      health food stores.

3.   Do not sit for long periods without changing positions. It
      is better if you can get up and move around every twenty
      minutes. Do not cross your legs at the knees. This is very
      bad for circulation. It is a hard habit to break but is
      possible with awareness and determination.

4.   Do some form of regular exercise every day. Swimming
      and vigorous walking are both good.

5.   While in the bath or shower, massage the cellulite area
      with a loofa (a coarse natural fiber), brush, or abrasive
      type sponge. It is not necessary to do this very hard, just
      enough to increase circulation. Actually, it is best to do
      this over your entire body, whenever you have the time.
          Whichever tool you choose to use should be well
      soaped so that it will run smoothly over the body. This
      regimen is very invigorating and will also promote
      healthier looking skin. Towel dry the body with upward,
      vigorous motions. After drying, massage the areas with
      lotion. This will also help alleviate the problem and
      replace any oil lost from the soap.

6.   Stop eating so much hard fat such as butter, cream, and
      meat fat. Eliminate bacon, ham, pork, and all fatty meat
      from your diet. Substitue this saturated fat with two or
      three tablespoons of cold pressed vegetable oil daily.
      Use peanut, safflower, sunflower or corn oil. Refrigerate
      the oil.

7. Start watching what you are putting into your body. Eat plenty of cleansing fresh fruits, juices, and vegetables. Try making a meal of one fruit like oranges, grapefruit, cantaloupe or watermelon. Eat as much as you like.

Congestion

Being congested can be very annoying. It can also be scary if breathing becomes difficult. Here are some suggestions to bring relief.

To one cup of boiling water, add two tablespoons of vinegar. Make a tent over the head with a towel, and inhale the fumes for a few minutes. Do this several times throughout the day until your lungs and nasal passages feel clear.

Follow this with a few drops of vitamin E oil in each nostril. This keeps nasal passages clear and prevents a cold from developing.

Pleurisy Root is very relieving for colds and congestion. You can purchase this herb at most health food stores in bulk form. Steep according to directions. Make at least a quart of the tea, and store in the refrigerator. Drink it either hot or cold several times a day until the congestion is gone. Honey may be added.

Constipation

Constipation should never be ignored. It is very important to good health to have regular bowel movements. If you use the following suggestions it could help you to have regular elimination.

Take one tablespoon of bran each morning in juice or water. Buy several kinds; oat bran, rice bran, and corn bran. This will allow you to rotate them and not become allergic to one kind. Once the body has developed good elimination habits, the bran may be reduced, or even stopped.

Eat lots of fresh fruits and vegetables. Chew your food slowly. DO NOT DRINK FLUIDS WITH YOUR MEALS.

Liquids tend to delute your degestive enzymes. Be sure to drink several glasses of water daily, but don't do it at meal time.

Cough

If you have a persistent cough that is interrupting your sleep, try this. Pin a cold, wet washcloth around the throat and cover with a dry cloth. Remove it in the morning, and be sure to rinse the outside of the throat with cold water to close the pores.

I always used this for my children when they had colds. They did not cough all night and were able to get their much needed rest.

Another remedy for night coughing is to drink comfrey tea, made either from the leaf or from tea bags. Honey may be added. This remedy is also curative, while the above remedy is only a relief. Comfrey is wonderful for asmthmatics and people with allergies. (See Allergies & Congestion above.)

Croup

This childhood cough can be very scary. Once a neighbor called for help with her toddler, who could hardly breathe. While she called a doctor who made house calls, I did the following:

I took the baby into the bathroom and turned on the hot water taps full force in both the shower and the basin. I then wrapped ice in a towel and put it around his throat. I had heard of people using snow for this purpose in the harsh midwest winters. By the time the doctor got there (about 15 minutes), the baby was breathing easier. The doctor said I did the right thing and probably saved the child's life.

Depression

Whenever you have been under any kind of stress - emotional problems, illness, or work pressures - you use up your B Vitamins. To alleviate this shortage, take one tablet of a good B Complex 50 or 75 balance each morning.

Eat steamed or raw green leafy vegetables, and organ meats, such as, heart, liver, and kidney. These foods are all rich in the B vitamins. Eating yogurt (low fat if you are watching your calories) provides the bacteria to synthesize the B vitamins in the intestines. Avoid junk food, and eat fresh fruit and nuts instead. Don't forget to be nice to yourself.

Diarrhea

Each time you have an attack of diarrhea, drink a glass of fresh fruit juice (without sugar). Add one half teaspoon of honey and a pinch of salt. Even if you have to do this every 15 minutes, do it. This prevents weakness and stops the attacks within a few hours. The juice helps replace the potassium lost in a diarrhea attack. That is what causes the weakness associated with it.

Another potassium-rich source is garlic. Try mashing six cloves of garlic and spread the mixture on bread with butter to help get it down. You may use garlic capsules if you prefer. Follow with a glass of warm water with two tablespoons of vinegar and two tablespoons of honey added. Vinegar helps your body absorb the potassium more quickly, and efficiently. The honey makes the vinegar more palitable, and gives energy. Use raw honey. This is honey that has not been processed, so it has more value. (The raw honey I use, is available at the super market and is probably less expensive than in the health food store.) This remedy usually works within 24 hours.

Ear Aches

Ear aches can be very painful. If a child has an ear ache (especially in the night) a parent can feel so helpless seeing him in terrible pain, and unable to sleep.

Garlic oil placed in the ear will usually bring relief within 15 minutes. Garlic has many natural healing powers without any side effects. Unless you want to call the odor a side effect. Puncture a garlic capsule with a sterile needle and put a few drops in the aching ear. Don't do this if you are planning a trip to your doctor. He won't be able to see the affected area if anything is in the ear.

Eye Irritation

For red, irritated or tired eyes try this soothing remedy: Steep one heaping teaspoon of Camomille tea in a cup of boiling water for five or six minutes. Store the cooled solution in a sterile, covered jar, and keep it in the refrigerator. Bathe or soak the affected eye with compresses several times a day. This is very soothing and relieving to red or irritated eyes. Be sure to see your doctor if it is serious or isn't better in a few hours. Camomille is available at most health food stores.

Fungus Inflamation

Fungus inflamation frequently occurs after taking an antibiotic, being under stress, or being ill. All the ointments in the world won't help unless your need for B vitamins is met and the good bacteria is restored.

Take a good B Complex, 50 or 75 balance. Eat plenty of green leafy vegetables, organ meats, and yogurt, and drink acidophilus milk. Put plain yogurt on the affected area and cover to protect clothing.

Gas & Bloating

Gas or bloating can usually be helped by some simple common sense methods. If these do not work, see a physican.

Eat smaller meals. Chew your food well. Eat slowly with no liquids before or during your meal. Don't eat if you are upset. Take a good B Complex 50 or 75 balance. After each of your 3 daily meals, take 50 to 100 MG of Panothanic Acid.

One of the B vitamins.

Here is a good example of a gastric problem solved simply. An engineer friend took his family for pizza every Wednesday evening. After their night out, just like clock work, he would wake up at 3:00 AM with gas and pain. Having a very analytical mind, (and several weeks of discomfort) he figured out why. While he and his family were waiting for their pizza to be served, he drank many glasses of ice water. When they returned home, he drank more water (probably from thirst caused by monosodium glutamate in the pizza). He said that as soon as he stopped drinking the water, he had no more trouble. The water was preventing his digestive enzymes from working.

Sometimes, as we grow older, our digestive enzymes get lazy and need a boost. Papaya enzyme tablets are helpful as an aid to digestion and are available in health food stores. Make certain the brand you choose is sugar-free. Fresh papaya or pineapple is also effective. Finish your meal with one of these succulent fruits.

Another remedy for gas is:
Steep ½ teaspoon of the herbs Golden Seal with ⅛ teaspoon of Myrrh in one cup of boiling water. Let it steep for about 15 minutes. After cooling, store it in the refrigerator. Take a *small sip* of the brew before each meal. It should prevent gas and bloating.

Hair Loss

Often, after a severe illness, working under pressure, or worrying, hair may fall out.

To correct this condition, you must first improve your diet. Eat protein and vitamin B rich foods. These include organ meats, yogurt, wheat germ, and Brewers yeast. Green leafy vegetables and lots of fresh fruits should also be included in your diet.

Get plenty of rest. Do something constructive about your

problem if your hair loss is due to worry. Worrying never solves anything, just compounds it.

Take a good B Complex 50 or 75 balance. Read the label and make sure it contains PABA, folic acid, biotin, and inosital. If you are graying, the inosital may help your hair return to its original color.

Chinese ginger is a good stimulant. Massage the ginger into your scalp each night. It is available at Chinese Herb Stores. (Also see Depression above.)

Headaches

Headaches can occur for many different reasons. Here are a few suggestions that could relieve the pain:

1. Mix the following in a blender: 6 ounces of non-fat milk, ¼ teaspoon brewers yeast, ½ tablespoon of soy lecithin granules, and four ounces of apple juice. Drink very slowly. You should feel relief in 10 to 15 minutes. This drink will also give you a nice lift as it increases your energy.

2. Massaging the webbed area between your thumb and forefinger of each hand, will sometimes relieve a head-ache. This procedure is also done to revive someone who has fainted. It is called acu-pressure and works on the same principle as acupuncture.

3. Some headaches are the result of low blood sugar. If this is the cause of your headache, eat five or six small meals daily. Make sure these meals include protein and Vitamin B rich foods such as liver, wheat germ and yeast.

4. Drinking peppermint tea is sometimes very relieving for headaches. If you don't have any peppermint (tea or oil)

on hand, use plain hot water with fresh lemon. Drink this
slowly and do not sweeten.

Hemorrhoids

Sometimes after having diarrhea, lifting heavy objects,
being constipated, or bearing a child, you can develop painful
hemorrhoids. For relief, grate a raw carrot or blenderize a half
cup of fresh cranberries. Wrap a tablespoon of it in a thin layer
of cloth or gauze and place over the affected area. Store the
remainder in the refrigerator.

Within one half hour, you should feel relief as the com-
press draws out the inflamation. Change the poltice every
hour if you do this during the day, otherwise leave it in place
all night. (Also read the remedy for Constipation, above.)

Another remedy that works well is using vitamin E
capsules. Keep the vitamin E stored in the refrigerator to
preserve its freshness. Puncture a capsule with a sterile
needle and insert the capsule into the rectum. A lubricant of
vasoline or vitamin E oil can be used for ease of insertion.
Then rub some vitamin E from another punctured capsule on
the outside area. Liquid vitamin E may be used for this. Do
this each morning and at bedtime, and do it faithfully It's
worth the effort. "Wipe" with a cool, wet cloth instead of toilet
paper. Toilet tissue is very abrasive. Splash Witch Hazel on a
piece of cotton for cleaning the area. It is refreshing, non-
irritating, and more economical than commercial wipes and is
available at most drug stores.

Taking Rutin also is a big help. Take at least 50 mgs. daily.
Rutin is very good for arteries in general. Check with your
doctor before taking anything new.

Hiccoughs

There are several methods for relieving this irritating
disfunction. Drink the juice of a fresh orange. This sometimes
stops hiccoughs. Eating a small quantity of blackboard chalk

is sometimes helpful.

A friend of mine wins bets with his remedy: Plug your ears, and drink water very slowly. (You will need the assistance of a friend here.)

Taking a spoonful of onion juice is most successful in stubborn cases of hiccoughs. Like garlic, onion juice has many powerful healing qualities.

Eating a spoonful of honey may also do the trick.

High Blood Pressure

There are some simple things you can do that could reduce this dangerous but often painless condition.

Take one to two tablespoons of soy lecithin granules daily.
Lecithin is rich in choline, which is needed to reduce high blood pressure. Keep the container tightly closed and in the refrigerator.

Also take one garlic capsule with each meal. This works very slowly to reduce blood pressure, so it is not a burden to your system. It sometimes raises low blood pressure to normal. Garlic also has a tendency to reduce the appetite, therefore an added benefit could be a possible weight loss, which would be doubly beneficial in reducing high blood pressure. Garlic does not interfere with any medication you might be taking because it is a food, not a drug.

Insect Bites and Stings

Any of the following herbs may be applied to relieve the itching and swelling associated with insect bites and stings: Sweet Basil, Fennel Plantain, or Scullcap. Steep a teaspoon of the herb in ½ cup of boiling water for 10 minutes. After the solution has cooled, soak a cloth in it and place on the affected area. Cover with a dry cloth. As the cloth dries out, replace it with a fresh one. Repeat this until the symtems are gone.

If you have an allergy to any insect bite or sting, carry 500 or 1000 mg. of vitamin C with you. If you are bitten, take one or two capsules every hour for several hours. This will lessen the discomfort. Ask your doctor about taking vitamin C.

Raw honey is also very relieving. Spread some on the bite, and cover with a cloth to protect clothing.

Insomnia

Next time you have trouble sleeping, instead of reaching for a drug, try any of the following:

1. There are several herbal teas that work very well to help you sleep, and they have no side effects. In fact, they are very good for your stomach. These herbs are usually available at most health food stores and include Hops, Catnip, Valerian, and Lady's Slipper. Follow the instructions on the label for best results and drink before retiring. After steeping, drink while the tea is still warm.

2. Have you ever lain awake thinking of all the things you wanted to accomplish the following day? Just keep a pad and pencil by your bed, and write down the things you want to remember to do. Once you have made this notation, it may be possible for your mind to relax and forget.

3. If your insomnia is caused from worry, close your eyes and relax. Concentrate on the images you see. Sometimes this alone will do the trick. I do this, and sometimes I see things like beautiful roses, feathers, brightly colored designs, or sculptured faces. You can not very well worry if you are thinking about something else. (See the section on Imagary)

4. If tense, or overly tired, try this:
    Close your eyes and picture some quiet place. Perhaps a wooded glade with a brook running close by.

Imagine the soothing sounds of water running over the rocks. You spot a giant leaf, and decide to use it for your raft. You push off from shore and lie down on your cozy bed which just fits your body. As you watch sunlight filter through the trees, your craft rocks gently as it carries you down the stream. You will probably be asleep before you get any further. Anyway, you get the general idea. I use this scenario to go to sleep whenever I can not relax. It has became like a conditioned reflex, I am asleep as soon as I "board my leaf." Maybe you have a special place you would like to use. You are only limited by your imagination.

5.   Reading a few pages in a book works for some people. A novel or some light reading is best. Freeing your mind is the secret.

6.   Excessive use of alcohol can cause insomnia. Alcohol sometimes makes you sleepy, but as it wears off, you tend to waken. (Instead of alcohol, try one of the herb teas listed in 1 above.)

7.   Eating late at night or overeating can keep you awake. (Try one of the herb teas listed in 1 above.)

8.   Eating sweets could keep you awake as sugar is very stimulating.

Joint Pain

There are a number of things that can be done to help relieve joint pain without using drugs. Here are some suggestions:

1.   Massaging joints with cold pressed peanut oil is very relieving. Rub the painful area with the oil once a day for

10 or 20 minutes. Do not wipe the oil off when you finish -
let it soak in. A good time to do this is in the evening while
watching TV or before going to bed. Keep the oil in the
refrigerator, and pour a small amount in a dish for your
massage. Use any of these oils: safflower, sunflower,
corn, or peanut, but make sure the oil you select is cold
pressed. Also be sure to protect clothing from the oil.

2.   Drink one tablespoon of the above mentioned cold
      pressed oils before each meal. This will help lubricate
      your joints and make your skin more youthful looking at
      the same time. The oil can be taken in juice or milk.

3.   Whenever you think of it, exercise the painful joint
      slowly and carefully, make circular motions. Keep the
      joint warm, and stay out of the wind. Do not drive with
      the car window open.

4.   There are two drinks that might be effective in relieving
      joint pain. One is Burdock Root, which is very purifying
      to the system, and the other is unsweetened cherry juice,
      which contains something naturally that seems to relieves
      inflamation. Either, or both of these drinks may be
      used.
          Drink two cups of Burdock Root tea daily. Steep one
      teaspoon in a cup of boiling water for six to ten minutes.
      Drink it while it is still warm.
          Drink a glass of unsweetened cherry juice, or eat
      fresh cherries when in season. Do this daily.

5.   Avoid all processed foods including: sugar, white flour,
      animal fats, alcohol, pork, and caffeine. Eat liver, yeast,
      and wheat germ, which are all rich in B vitamins. Also eat
      plenty of fresh fruit and green leafy vegetables every
      day, and take a good B Complex 50 or 75 balance. Ask

your doctor about taking a calcium/magnesium
supplement.

6.   Sometimes painful joints occur because we suppress
      anger. Put a pillow in a corner and kick it, or beat your
      fists on a stack of pillows. Get out in the country and
      holler. See a comedy that will make you laugh loudly.
      There is nothing like a good belly-laugh to make you feel
      fit.

Low Blood Sugar
Listed below are some things to do, and not to do, that may
help to keep you blood sugar from dropping. Check with your
doctor or health care specialist before taking any of these
supplements.

DO'S
1.   Take one tablespoon of cold pressed peanut oil before
      each meal. The oil slows down the emptying process in
      the stomach, and also works as a catalyst to burn the
      saturated fats in your body. This enables the blood sugar
      to stay at a normal level for longer periods.

2.   Eat five or six small meals, rather than three large ones.
      Each meal should include protein and vitamin B rich
      foods like liver, yeast, and wheat germ.

3.   Keep potassium tablets with you at all times. If you can't
      eat at the proper time, take one tablet. Low blood sugar
      causes loss of potassium through urine. First, ask your
      doctor about taking a potassium supplement.

4.   Take a good B Complex 50 or 75 balance each morning
      with breakfast. This will help relieve the stress of low
      blood sugar and increase the needed pantothenic acid

which is in short supply when low blood sugar is present.

5.   Take a C Complex three or four times during the day. I
     take 2000 mg. with each meal and at bedtime. I in-
     creased the amount gradually, starting with 100 mg.

     If vitamin C causes diarrhea, it is usually due to the
     filler used in the tablet, not the C. Buy only a small
     quantity to start with, to see if that type agrees with you.
     Talk to your doctor about what vitamin C you should
     take.

     I prefer the capsule rather then the tablet which
     remains in the stomach in one piece. If you have ever
     held a vitamin C tablet in your mouth, then you know
     how strong the acidity is. If you do decide to buy
     capsules, make sure they are in a tamper-proof container.

     The only place I have been able to find the C
     Complex 1000 mg. capsule is at the General Nutrition
     Stores (GNC). These stores are located in most cities
     and towns throughout the United States.

DON'TS
1.   Don't eat sugar or artificial sweeteners. They both have
     a tendency to raise blood sugar very high, and then it
     drops very low.

2.   Don't skip meals, and try to eat before you get too
     hungry.

3.   Don't drink coffee, tea with caffeine, colas, or alcohol.

Menopause
Many women have very little trouble when they reach this
stage in life if their diet is adequate. As the reproductive
organs start slowing down, the need for vitamin E and calcium
increases. Due to the stress associated with hot flashes, night

sweats, worry over growing old, irritability, and insomnia, the need for B vitamins also increases.

There is a product called Bioplasma 6X. It is made up of a combination of 12 ingredients that stimulate the tissue salts in the body. It is a homoeopathic formula (only natural ingredients), and can help to relieve some of the unwanted symptoms of menopause. It is available at most health food stores. Ask your physican about taking this supplement.

Find a good nutritionist to evaluate your situation and recommend appropriate vitamins and minerals in the proper dosage for your special needs. He or she will help you plan a diet rich in all the nutrients necessary to help you feel good again. You may even feel better than you ever felt before.

Menstrual Cramps

When my daughter was in college, she started having monthly cramps. She was so busy with her new schedule that she hadn't been drinking her usual three or four glasses of milk each day. When she realized that she wasn't getting enough calcium, she started taking four calcium/magnesium tablets daily. It was only two days later that her period started but this time there were no cramps. In fact, she was never bothered with cramps again. Therefore, drink a quart of milk each day or take a calcium/magnesium supplement. A balance of at least half as much magnesium as calcium should be taken. Check with your doctor before taking these minerals.

Many people cannot tolerate milk, so it is essential to get calcium from other sources. Bones are a good source. Save them from chicken, turkey, beef, lamb, or any other bones from your meals. Freeze them and when you have enough, place them in a kettle and cover with cold water. Cook very slowly (simmer) for about two hours. Make sure the lid fits tightly. When the stock is cool, remove the bones, skim the fat, and store the stock in the freezer. When you make soup, the stock will provide a nourishing base. You need only add fresh vegetables, grains, and herbs to have a hearty soup that is rich in calcium. The following makes a delicious soup:

VEGETABLE RICE SOUP
To 2 quarts of stock add:
Any meat that was left on the bones (diced)
½ cup uncooked brown rice
1 cup of sliced carrots
½ cup of chopped celery
1 cup of roughly sliced cabbage
1 chopped onion
1 cup frozen mixed vegetables or any leftover
vegetables
1 16 oz. can tomatoes
1 bay leaf

Simmer the meat and rice in a large heavy pot while preparing the vegetables. Make sure that the pot is covered and that the stock simmers slowly. Add the other ingredients as they are prepared in the order listed above. Simmer only long enough to be tender. Do not let the soup boil. Remove the bay leaf and let the soup cool. It will be thick, actually more like a stew. Add more liquid if you like.

Store all but enough for one meal in plastic jars labeled with date and type of soup, and put in the freezer. Leave enough room in each jar for expansion when frozen. Defrost in the microwave or thaw ahead of time. Add salt and pepper to taste. This hearty soup will make a nice meal when accompanied by a salad, whole grain bread or muffins, and fruit.

Another nourishing, delicious soup that provides a good source of calcium is:

TURKEY LENTIL SOUP
Place in a kettle:
3 qts. water
1 turkey leg, with skin removed
2 cups lentils, rinsed and drained
1 large onion, minced
1 large carrot, sliced
3 stalks of celery, including tops
1 sprig of parsley

Cover and simmer for four or five hours, or until lentils are tender. Remove the turkey leg, and throw away the bone. Dice the turkey meat, and return it to the pot. Just before serving, add salt and pepper to taste and one tablespoon of vinegar. (See above soup recipe for storage directions.)

Of course, cramps could be caused by something other than a calcium deficiency, so always check with your health care specialist if the above remedies don't work for you.

Nose Irritations

For minor irritation or dryness in the nose, try this: Steep 1 teaspoon of Golden Seal (an herb available at most health food stores) in a cup of boiling water for 15 or 20 minutes. After cooling, strain into a sterile jar, cover, and place in the refrigerator. Each morning and evening, take about a teaspoon of the tea, and gently sniff into each nostril. It works very well if you are not using any medication. If your condition doesn't improve, see your doctor, and ask him to take a nose culture.

Incidentally, Golden Seal is also an excellent mouth and throat gargle.

Overweight

There is no substitute for eating properly. If we ate the

proper foods in the correct amounts, we would, in most cases, not have a weight problem. Here are some ideas that do work for losing weight. These suggestion can be used alone or in combination.

a)   Fennel tea may help reduce your appetite. Drink two cups each day. Steep 1½ teaspoons of Fennel seeds for six to ten minutes. It has a pleasant taste, similar to licorice. Fennel seeds are available at most health food stores.

b)   Cider vinegar helps to change your PH balance (from alkaline to acid), which in turn helps you to lose weight. Use one or two tablespoons of vinegar, and ½ teaspoon of honey, stirred into a cup of hot water before breakfast. Drink slowly. Rinse your mouth with clear water when finished. Vinegar is not good for teeth. You may want to substitue lemon for the vinegar as it works on the same principle.

c)   For a diet breakfast, try this tasty, energizing drink. It is a great way to start the morning.

Mix in the blender: * Refrigerate
½ banana   2 tablespoons protein
2 or 3 fresh strawberries,   powder. (I prefer the ones
a slice of fresh pineapple,   made from eggs & milk
or any other fresh fruit.   not the soya base.)
* 1 tablespoon lecithin   ¼ teaspoon Brewers Yeast
* 1 teaspoon wheat germ   * 1 tablespoon aloe vera
* 1 tablespoon vetetable   gel
   oil   ½ cup unsweetened pine-
½ teaspoon alfalfa seeds.   apple juice (substitute
2 heaping tablespoons of   any unsweetened juice or

(continued next page)

Mix in blender: *Refrigerate
* yogurt   combine 2 or 3 juices)
(I like plain Dannon)
½ cup low fat milk

This drink is satisfying and should easily support you until mid-day. Sometimes I drink it for lunch also and have a small dinner consisting of fish or chicken with vegetables or a salad. If you would like to have this drink for lunch also, make enough in the morning for two servings, and store the second half in a thermos that has been chilled before filling.

When you purchase protein powder, read the label. See that it has at least 24 grams of protein per two tablespoons.

d)   If you get hungry for bread or something sweet, try my Oat Flowers. I call them Flowers because they don't have any flour, only the tempting bouquet of good food. This recipe makes 12 muffins. After baking and cooling, store in the freezer. When desired, you may pop one in the microwave oven for 10 or 15 seconds. Of course they can also be heated in a conventional oven.

OAT FLOWERS

In a large bowl mix: In a small bowl mix:
2¼ cups oat bran   1 ripe, mashed, banana
1 tablespoon baking   2 eggs, beaten
powder   1 teaspoon Vanilla
A dash of salt   ⅓ cup non-fat milk
¼ cup raisins   (Add to other ingred-
¼ cup raw sunflower seeds   ients and mix thor-
(keep in the freezer)   oughly.)
2 tablespoons vegetable oil
(keep in the refrigerator)

4 tablespoons or less, raw
honey
4 tablespoons or less,
molasses

Spoon into muffin tin lined with cupcake papers.
Bake at 400 degrees for 15-18 minutes. When cool, place
them in a plastic bag and store in the freezer.

e)   There are two amino acids that help me appease my
     appetite. One is L-Phenylalanine, which makes me feel
     less hungry, and the other is L-Glutamine, which sus-
     tains my blood sugar level. I take 250 mg. of the L-
     Phenylalanine and 500 mg. of the L-Glutamine on an
     empty stomach when I first get up in the morning and the
     same amount again an hour before lunch.
        Don't do this if you have high blood pressure, are
     pregnant, do not have your full growth, or are a diabetic.
     Be sure to check with your doctor first. If you decide to
     take any amino acids HAVE YOUR BLOOD PRES-
     SURE CHECKED OFTEN. Some amino acids have a
     tendency to raise blood pressure, and must be moni-
     tored often.

f)   It's always hardest for me not to eat in the evening when
     watching TV. One thing that helps is keeping my hands
     busy, but one can only make so many hooked rugs. I have
     solved this problem with fruit juice popcicles. In a quart
     jar, I mix several naturally sweetened juices, usually
     papaya juice, pineapple juice, cherry cider and apple
     juice. They may also be mixed in the blender along with
     fresh fruit. Use your imagination while keeping the
     calories to a minimum. After blending, place the mixture
     in plastic popcicle holders, small containers, or ice trays
     with toothpick handles. Fruitcicles are quite satisfying,

and I am still going to bed with a fairly empty stomach.

g)   Don't skip meals. Eat a good breakfast and lunch, which
     will keep blood sugar up so appetite will not accelerate
     as the day progresses.
         Your biggest meal should be breakfast. Lunch and
     dinner should be progressively lighter meals. Try to go
     to bed with an empty stomach. Eat nothing after 6 PM as
     you will not burn off the calories before retiring.

h)   When ordering salad while dining out, request the
     dressing on the side. In this way, you can control the
     calorie amount by not using more than is necessary.
         Speaking of dressings, if you order oil and vinegar,
     make an effort to determine if the dressing has been
     properly refrigerated. Does it smell fresh? Is the bottle
     chilled or warm? Ask the waiter if the dressing has been
     chilled. Recently, while dining in a very fine restaurant, I
     was served rancid oil for my salad. As I looked around
     the dining room, I could see a serving table storing
     bottles of oil, and they were not chilled.

i)   Get some kind of exercise each day. Walking for ½ hour
     twice daily is great. Join a volley ball or soft ball team.
     Take tap dancing lessons; if this is too strenuous, try
     ballroom dancing lessons, and practice often by getting
     out in the evenings where live music is provided. It's so
     much more fun than that old "boob tube."
         If you have a sedentary job, get out of your chair
     often. Do not save up chores to do all at once - go make
     that copy, check the mail room, visit that other depart-
     ment instead of using the phone. If you spend long hours
     on the phone, it might be worth while to get an extension
     cord so that you can get up and move around while
     talking. A stock broker friend does this because she

spends so many inactive hours at her desk. Now she paces back and forth while making her calls.

Whenever you can, use the office stairs instead of the elevator. Park at the far end of the parking lot, if it is well lighted and safe.

Take a light lunch with a hard boiled egg or cold chicken and fresh fruits and raw vegetables. If there is no refrigeration at work, include a sealed plastic container of ice to keep your lunch fresh without worry of bacteria building up. Interest some friends in walking with you after lunch. This makes it fun, and you will help keep each other enthused. You will mutually enjoy seeing the results of weight loss, added energy, and a glowing sense of well being.

In the evening, do some of your TV watching on the floor while exercising. It beats eating. It actually makes you less hungry and less tired. This is especially helpful if you have to go to an evening meeting or class.

When you visit a shopping mall, park in one place and walk to all of your destinations. If you have to make trips back to your car to unload, so much the better. Make sure the place you choose to park is safe and well lighted.

If you have a child, play with him or her for an hour each day. When I say play, I mean on the child's level. Do everything he does. Get on the floor with him, run, climb, and jump. Bring out the child in yourself. It is a great way to get a good workout while you are getting closer to your child. It should be fun for you both.

Be aware of how good moving around is for your body, and take the long way whenever possible. You'll see for yourself, very soon, when you get rid of the sluggishness and replace it with vitality and a zest for living.

While you are losing weight, your stomach will start

getting flatter, as you eat less and exercise more. Here is
a little secret that comes from China; it will help flatten
your tummy faster. Lie flat on your back (on the bed or
floor). Take the palm of your right hand and massage, or
rather gently push the skin across your stomach toward
the left side of your body. Do this for ten or fifteen
minutes each day.

Pregnancy

This very special time can be more enjoyable. Listed
below are some suggestions to make your months in waiting,
and the recovery period afterward, a little more pleasant,
comfortable, and healthy:

1.   Drink a cup of Red Rasberry tea (made from the leaves)
     each day. It is healthful and strengthening. It will lessen
     any morning sickness and reduce labor discomfort.
     American Indian women did this and were noted for
     having easy deliveries.

2.   Have a regular exercise program. Don't over exert. Walk
     in the fresh air every day, taking deep breaths. Swim as
     long as the doctor and the weather allow. It is very
     important to keep muscles strong and toned.

3.   Wear support hose to protect your legs. The added
     weight during pregnancy could cause varicose veins, and
     the stockings can help to prevent this. As you gain more
     weight, put the stockings on before getting out of bed
     each morning. This way, you will gain the full benefit
     from the stockings before putting any pressure on your
     legs and veins.

4.   Eat simple, nourishing meals which include a variety of
     fresh fruits and vegetables. Meat is very hard on already-

taxed kidneys. Eat meat only as a condiment, but be sure to get enough protein from other sources, such as cheese, milk, nuts, seeds, and cottege cheese.

5. Remember that you are literally molding a new life. If you want your baby to be relaxed and happy, you must be relaxed and happy. If you feel tense, try singing; your baby will like that. Do deep breathing exercises outdoors or in front of an open window; it's good for relaxing.

6. If you have an episiotomy (childbirth incision), try this for comfort, cleanliness, and faster healing after returning home from the hospital:

    Place a large package of 4x4 sterile guaze squares (or make your own) in a sterile jar. Cover with Witch Hazel (available at your local drug store). Keep this covered jar handy in the bathroom. Each time you make a trip there, place one of these wet, guaze, squares on the inside of your sanitary napkin. It is very refreshing. Some hospitals provide this service for their new mothers.

7. Plenty of rest is very important after your baby is born. Do not do anything for two weeks. Give your body a chance to heal and return to normal. Your needs and your baby's needs are all that are important.

8. Bind your stomach using an old sheet. They might do this in the hospital if you request it. It may sound old fashioned, but you won't think so when your stomach returns to normal. Some young women have stomachs that look like deflated balloons. Massaging your stomach with vitamin E oil is very helpful and stimulating to the area. The vitamin E will also help reduce stretch marks.

9. If you are nursing your baby, continue the simple diet
    (see 3 above). Drink at least six glasses of water each day
    to help increase milk supply. Keep calm. If you get upset,
    it will decrease your milk supply. Conversely, if you take
    brewer's yeast daily, it will increase your milk and help to
    keep you calm. Ask your doctor about taking brewer's
    yeast.

10. Toughen up nipples to prepare for nursing by rubbing
    gently with a coarse wash cloth and then massaging with
    vitamin E after drying. Do this daily. Otherwise, nursing
    can be very painful at first. Don't spoil this wonderful
    experience by not being prepared.

11. After you have gradually weaned your baby, drink Sage
    tea, and cut down on your fluid intake to reduce the milk
    flow.

12. Start exercising as soon as you get approval from your
    doctor. Take walks in the fresh air to build your strength
    and keep your muscles toned.

13. When I was carrying my first child, I read a book that had
    a profound effect on my life. It eliminated all labor, and
    pain and discomfort in general. The book, "Childbirth
    Without Fear" by Dr. Grantly Dick-Read, and published
    by Harper, is still very popular today. I had no labor to
    speak of. Since reading the book, I have never been
    fearful of the dentist, and it has never been necessary for
    me to require novacaine or any painkiller. The book is
    available at most libraries.

Prostate Problems

A friend of mine thought that he had strained himself
while moving to a new home, but his physican diagnosed that

it was his prostate. The doctor told him he would probably need surgery eventually. I gave him some zinc tablets and recommended he take 15 mgs daily, and he has never had any further discomfort. That was 10 years ago.

It seems that 98% of older men get some kind of prostate problem because they don't get enough zinc in their diet. Check with your doctor first.

Rectal Itching

Rectal itching can be very uncomforable. Try the following for relief:

Place a piece of guaze or cotton soaked with vinegar over the area; change it each time you go to the bathroom. If the skin is broken, it may sting at first, but it will relieve the itching. Vitamin E rubbed gently on the area will also help provide relief. (See Hemorrhoids above.)

Scarring

Normally, when we think of scars, we think of external marks from injuries or burns, but scarring occurs inside the body as well. Internal scarring can occur from smoking, nitrites, excess alcohol, pnuemonia, or surgery, just to name a few of the reasons.

Taking vitamin E supplements can help reduce the internal scarring as well as scars on the skin surface. Massaging the scarred skin with vitamin E oil is very helpful if done consistantly. Keep the vitamin E in the refrigerator when not in use. Eating all the proper nutrients also helps restore the tissue to normal. Ask your doctor about taking a supplement.

Skin, Dry

Every year people spend millions of dollars on creams, lotions, and treatments for dry skin. These usually expensive concoctions only provide temporary surface relief and do not really solve the problem. Dry skin must be treated from within. Following are suggestions to improve your skin tone at any age and promote a vibrant, youthful, complexion.

1.   Take at least one tablespoon of cold pressed peanut oil with each meal. The oil can be taken alone, in juice, skim milk, or on salad.

Our natural skin oils are unsaturated and, it is believed, made of essential fatty acids, so oils in the diet are required. Taking these oils also provide necessary vitamin E. People who have been on oil-free diets over a long period of time usually have very dry skin.

Be sure to keep the oil refrigerated and tightly capped. This will keep it fresh longer and prevent rancidity.

2.   Take a tablespoon of cod liver oil at bedtime. After taking this amount for several weeks, you may be able to reduce the daily dose to twice weekly instead. Use your ear wax consistency as a guage. When the wax becomes soft, you will know it is time to reduce the amount of oil.

Use an emulsified cod liver oil. I particularly like Dale Alexander's Cod Liver Oil. This oil is very easy to take and leaves no after taste. Keep it tightly capped and refrigerated. This oil will give you the much needed vitamins A and D. When these vitamins are obtained from natural fish oils they are less toxic. Make sure you are not getting more vitamin A and D from other sources such as vitamins, or a multiple vitamin, while taking the cod liver oil, unless you have the approval of a physican.

3.   Take a B Complex 50 or 75 balance. One of the major causes of dry or oily skin is the lack of some of the B vitamins. (See The Thesaurus of Vitamins.)

4.   Vitamin C deficiency is another reason for abnormal
      skin moisture. Eat citrus fruits, and consider taking a
      vitamin C Complex supplement. Ask your doctor about
      the amount that would be best for you.

5.   When you are in the sun, use a good sun screen. Do not
      bake for hours during the heat of the day. Today's great
      looking tan will turn into dry, wrinkled, leathery skin
      later. If you are careful, your skin will stay youthful
      looking throughout your entire life. If you are older, say
      past forty, check a place on your body that has never
      been exposed to the elements. Notice how much softer,
      smoother, and wrinkle-free the area is.

6.   Drink several glasses of water, juice, and herbal teas
      each day. This will cleanse your system of toxic wastes
      and improve circulation.

7.   Make sure that your diet is adequate. Eat fresh fruits,
      vegetables, fish, chicken, lean meats, organ meats, milk
      and milk products, eggs, and whole grains.

Ulcers or Nervous Stomach

Here are some simple suggestions that could help in repairing an ulcer or clearing up the nervous stomach, which
could be the forerunner of an ulcer.

Drink Comfrey tea, which is very healing to the stomach. It
is available at most health food stores in bulk or bags. You can
also buy a Comfrey plant and use the leaves. Steep a tea-
spoonful of the bulk or use one tea bag several times each
day.

Ulcers are only a symptom; stress could be the problem.
Determine if something is bothering you, and see if you can
change it. If you cannot correct the situation, try to adjust and
learn to handle it. Take a good B Complex 50 or 75 balance to

help relieve the stress. Be sure to see a physican if the pain persists.

Vaginal Yeast

Vaginal yeast is an uncomfortable disorder that occurs sometimes after a woman has taken an antibiotic or has been under stress. To provide relief, carefully insert plain yogurt with a plastic applicator (purchased from your local drugstore and follow the enclosed directions). Do this every night at bedtime until all the symptoms are gone. Take a good B Complex 50 or 75 balance, and eat at least ½ cup of plain yogurt with fruit each day.

Because there is an ingredient in vinegar that kills yeast, a vinegar douche taken twice daily will provide relief. Use one tablespoon of vinegar to a quart of warm water.

Make sure that you have only a yeast infection. See your physican for a diagnosis.

Varicose Veins Prevention & Improvement

There are several reasons for varicose veins, including: heredity, constipation, obesity, sitting and standing for long periods, clots, and pregnancy.

The following suggestions can help reduce your chances of getting this sometimes serious ailment and possibly improve an existing condition.

1.   The bowels must be kept open (see Constipation above.) Do not sit on the toilet for long periods, reading and/or straining. This position slows the circulation of blood between the legs and heart.

2.   Don't wear tight fitting clothing. It prevents proper blood circulation.

3.   If you must sit much of the time, take a break and walk, or

get your feet up higher than your heart.

4.   If you must stand much of the time, walk or jog in place.
      Wear support hose on the job. That is what smart
      stewardesses, nurses, and beauticians do.

5.   Make sure your diet is adequate, and drink lots of fluids.
      Vitamin B Complex, C, and E are very helpful.

6.   Swimming, walking, and cool showers are all good for
      circulation. When in the bath or shower, rub your whole
      body (especially your legs) with a loofa or course sponge
      designed for that purpose. Use a mild soap and a circular
      motion. This will rid you of dry skin while you are in-
      creasing circulation.

7.   Being overweight can also put a strain on the veins,
      especially during pregnancy. Try to maintain the weight
      suggested by your doctor during this period.

Vision
    Farsightedness can sometimes be improved by eating raw
sunflower seeds. Eat a tablespoon full five or six times daily.
Keep the seeds tightly closed in a jar in the freezer. The seeds
also make your skin more soft and moist.
    Nearsightedness and night blindness can be caused by a
lack of vitamin A. To make up for vitamin A deficiency, eat
foods such as carrots, sweet potatoes, sqaush, spinach,
cauliflower, turnip greens, chard, collards, peaches, cherries,
papaya, cantaloup, persimmon, prunes, yellow corn meal, and
natural cheddar cheese.
    Ask your doctor about taking a supplement. Remember
that Vitamin A is toxic if too much is ingested. Carotene is a
good source of vitamin A and considered to be non-toxic.

Warts

Unsightly warts can usually be cured without surgery. Rub the wart with vitamin E daily. It will take about three weeks of consistent treatment before the wart starts to disappear. Eat plenty of vitamin A rich foods every day. (See Vision, above.)

Water Retention

Many people believe that drinking fluids causes fluid retention. This is not true. Drinking water is very cleansing to the entire system and may help prevent edema (swelling or water retention.)

If you suffer from swollen ankles, hands, or stomach, reduce your sodium intake. This includes salt, soda crackers, soft drinks, and any baked items that contain baking soda.

Watermelon is a natural diuretic without any side effects. Make a meal of this succulant fruit, and watch the swelling disappear.

Drink cleansing herbal teas such as Comfrey and Burdock Root.

A Vitamin B-6 deficiency can cause edema. Take a good B Complex 50 or 75 balance.

You have probably noticed that I have stressed a B Complex throughout the remedies. They are so important in any illness and really help in returning to good health more quickly.

Wrinkles & Aging

The best way to keep "Old Man Time" away from your door is to eat properly and not in excess, exercise regularly, be happy, and take a vital interest in life.

Listed below are some suggestions which could slow down or even reverse the aging process and prevent dry, wrinkled skin, fatigue, irritability, apathy, aching joints, and mental disorders.

1. **Nutrition**
    The better your nutrition, the more your body is able
    to fight disease. As you get older, less fat is needed, and
    more protein (from milk, lean meat, fish, and poultry) is
    required. This does not mean you need more food - only
    more nutrients. Eating less is usually better.
    Eat foods rich in nucleic acid (the basic building cell).
    These foods include fish (especially sardines); organ
    meats, such as sweetbread, liver heart, and kidney;
    brewer's yeast; and celery, radishes, onions, and beets.
    Try to eat fish at least once a day and sardines at least
    twice a week. Include all the other nucleic acid-rich
    foods as often as possible. Drink several glasses of water
    daily.

    After practicing this regimen for several weeks, you
    will be pleased to notice the backs of your hands looking
    younger, perhaps fewer wrinkles. When you awaken in
    the morning,your face will feel moist and vibrant, not oily
    or dry. Gradually, lines in your face and on your whole
    body will begin to lessen. If you follow this faithfully, the
    lines may disappear.

    By eating these foods, you will increase bile supply,
    which will help utilize the fat soluble vitamins A, D, and
    E, which in turn will help prevent infection by making
    your liver more efficient. Nucleic acid-rich foods should
    be easy to incorporate into your diet either at home or
    away. If you are watching your weight, these are excellent
    foods because they are low in calories and high in protein
    and other nutrients.

    When my children were growing up, I liked serving
    them liver at least once a week. My son Jeff was not a
    fussy eater, but he hated liver. Instead of fixing liver and
    onions I found a way to prepare it so that even he looked
    forward to having it on the menu. This is how I prepared
    it:

1 pound of calf liver
1 Bermuda onion
2-3 tablespoons mayonnaise
1 egg - hard boiled, peeled and chopped
Salt to taste

Use a heavy sauce pan with a lid. Cover the washed liver with water and simmer until all the redness is gone and the meat is tender, about 45 minutes. Drain and cool and put through the grinder. (You can substitute a heavy duty blender or chop the tender liver finely.) Next, grind the peeled onion. This will also clear all of the liver from the grinder, so none is wasted. Add the egg, mayonnaise and salt. Cover, and chill in the refrigerator. Serve on crackers, bread, celery, as a dip, or on lettuce leaves. Many people who never liked liver before, discover that they love it prepared this way.

As mentioned many times throughout this book, *the vitamins* play a very important part in good health. They are especially important as people get older.

(See Thesaurus of Vitamins for more information.) **Calcium** can protect you from osteoporosis (bone loss), help you to sleep more soundly, reduce pain, help your heart beat properly, and give you a feeling of well being.

As you get older, your need for calcium increases. Some good sources of this important mineral include: skim milk, nuts, collards, kale, turnip tops, dry beans, and soup made from bones. When steaming vegetables, save the nutrient rich water and drink it when cool.

If you decide to take a calcium supplement, be sure you take at least one half as much magnesium with it. It is possible to have a chemical imbalance if the two minerals are not taken together. There are calcium supplements which include other minerals and vitamin D all in the proper balance for good utilization. In any case, check with your doctor first.

Increase your intake of vitamin C. Eat fresh citrus fruits, and consider taking a vitamin C supplement. This will help protect you from environmental exposures like lead, DDT, and other toxic poisons such as food additives. Vitamin C will help fight infection, give you healthier gums, connecting tissues and increase your energy level.

Some authorities believe that vitamin E is the single most important preventative of aging. It is thought to improve blood circulation; prevent cataracts and other eye problems; relieve fatigue, and menopausal discomforts, and prevent testicle degeneration, leg cramps, and scarring (both internal and external).

The following foods contain this vital vitamin: cold pressed vegetable oils, wheat germ, soybean oil, cold pressed safflower oil, seeds, eggs, leafy vegetables, beef liver, meat, milk, nuts (raw), molasses, peanuts, legumes (peas, beans lentils), and unrefined cereal products.

Include a tablespoon of peanut oil before each meal. This will decrease your appetite while supplying you with vitamin E rich oil. Be sure the oil is tightly closed and in the refrigerator when not in use. Air and heat destroy the value of the oil, and it becomes rancid very easily, so don't leave it sitting out, or incapped any longer than necessary.

If you decide to take a vitamin E supplement, start with a very small amount, such as 100 mg. a day, which you can increase gradually over a period of weeks. If you get too much, it can make the corners of your mouth sore. Ask your doctor about the proper dosage for you.

2.   **Other Factors**

Some wise person once said that man must have three things to be complete - something to do, someone to love, and something to hope for.

a)   You can retire from a job, but you can't retire from
       life! At least not if you want to keep living.
       Remember all the things you wanted to do but
       never had time for while you were so busy raising a
       family, or making a living? Well, NOW is the time.
       Learn to play the piano, paint, read, write a book,
       fish or travel. Study; learn more about anything you
       are interested in. If you are an expert in some field
       become a consultant. Don't let your years of ex-
       perience go to waste; you may really have some-
       thing to contribute. Visit the museums, art galleries,
       zoo, beach, woods, or library. Join a club. There are
       so many senior clubs that not only have social
       functions, but actually help in finding agencies to
       aid in solving your special problems. Some older
       people say they don't want to be around other "old"
       people because they aren't young enough for them.
       Somehow, I think this is probably a cop-out for not
       getting out and about. At any age, a lot of people are
       afraid of the unknown. Then, when they finally do
       something different, they wonder why they didn't
       do it long ago. People that are out and doing are the
       ones that stay young longer.

b)   There are so many people and animals that need
       love. Befriend a lonely child, donate some time to
       your local nursing home or hospital, or - if your
       budget allows - get an animal. Even a small pet such
       as a canary can bring many hours of joy. Help out at
       your local elementary school. You might be re-
       sponsible for a child learning to read or taking a
       special interest in some sport.

c)   Set goals so you can be excited about the future. Be
       good to yourself by doing what you want to do (as
       long as it is constructive). Forget your chronological

age, and enjoy yourself. Remember that growing old is better than the alternative!

d)   Get some kind of exercise every day. Even if it is only a walk down the hall, it is a start. If you are in good health, take longer walks, swim, or work out at a gym. However, don't overdo and spoil the fun.

Exercise is so important. After 30 it becomes harder to extract oxygen from the air. Each year it becomes more difficult, but exercising helps slow the rate of decline.

III. SOURCES OF VITAMINS, MINERALS, AND HERBS

I find it less expensive to order vitamins, minerals, and herbs by mail. I also use local health food stores when I run short of something or can't locate special items. Mail order viatmins, minerals, and herbs have been very satisfactory, and the products are all guaranteed.

However, if price is not your first consideration, some of the local health food stores are operated by knowledgeable people who can answer some of your questions. I feel very fortunate in having a local health food store where the owner/manager is very knowledgeable and dedicated to providing his customers with detailed information about health and nutrition.

Your daily vitamins can be sorted for a week or two at one time. While preparing them, make a note of what you need. I like looking through catalogs, comparing prices, and ordering by phone, instead of standing in line at the store.

Most of the time, some of the companies listed below are having a two, or three, for one sale. Plan your buying so most of your purchases can be made during the sales.

These companies all have toll free 800 phone numbers that are convenient if you have a credit card. Some of them provide postage free envelopes for your orders and deliver free if you meet the minimum purchase amount. They will gladly send you a catalog if you call the 800 number. Listed below are a few that I use:

Consumer Vitamin Values (CVV)
860 Grand Blvd.

P.O. Box T
Deer Park, New York 11729-0919
800-645-5856
800-832-5865 (N.Y. Residents)
No shipping charges on orders over $15.00

Nature Food Centres
One Nature's Way
Wilmington, Mass 01887
800-225-0857
617-657-5000 (Mass. Residents)
No shipping charges on orders over $10.00

Puritan's Pride
105 Orville Drive
Bohemia, New York 11716-9986
800-645-1030 Ext. 130
800-832-1111 Ext. 130 (N.Y. Residents)
Open 8AM to Midnight EST. Mon. thru Sat.
No shipping charge on orders over $12.00

Vitamin Research Products
2044-A Old Middlefield Way
Mountain View, Ca. 94042
800-541-1623
800-541-8536 (Ca. Residents)
Will ship within 24 hours

Vitamin Research, in my estimation, is the Cadillac of the mail order vitamin companies. They have a customer service department to answer questions. They hold seminars and have a news letter. Vitamin Research donates a percent of their gross sales to research. Their sales are mostly introductory type. Any products may be tried and returned if you are not satisfied.

IV. A THESAURUS OF VITAMINS & MINERALS

Somehow, most people do not equate how they feel with what they put into their bodies. The following descriptions will help you understand the vital role that vitamins and minerals play in good health. You will be able to see what nutrients enhance each other, what works against them, in what foods these nutrients can be found, what parts of the body are affected, deficiency symtoms, and some therapeutic applications used.

THE FOLLOWING INFORMATION IS ONLY TO BE USED TO GAIN A BETTER UNDERSTANDING OF VITAMINS AND MINERALS. IT IS NOT MEANT FOR TREATMENT OR DIAGNOSIS OF ILLNESS.

THE USE OF CERTAIN DIETARY SUPPLEMENTS MAY RESULT IN ALLERGIC REACTION IN SOME INDIVIDUALS. CONSULT YOUR PHYSICAN BEFORE STARTING ANY REGIMEN. THIS INFORMATION IS NOT INTENDED TO BE DIAGNOSTIC OR PRESCRIPTIVE.

Key:
* essential for proper function
** equal dosage required
IU - International Units
Mg - Milligrams
Mcg - Micrograms

VITAMINS

MINERALS

VITAMIN A

Fat Soluble

Complementing Nutrients
B complex, choline, C, D, E*, F, calcium, phosphorus, zinc.

Anti-Vitamins
Alcohol, coffee, cortisone, excessive iron, mineral oil, vitamin D deficiency.

Sources
Green & yellow fruits & vegetables, milk, milk products, fish liver oil.

Apricots (dried) - 1 cup	16,000 IU
Liver (beef) - ¼ pound	50,000 IU
Spinach (cooked) - 1 cup	8,000 IU
Carrots (raw) - 1 medium	10,000 IU

Bodily Parts Affected
Bones, eyes, hair, skin, soft tissue, teeth.

Bodily Functions Facilitated
Body tissue reparation & maintenance (resist infection), visual purple production (necessary for night vision).

Deficiency Symtoms
Allergies, appetite loss, blemishes, dry hair, fatigue, itching/burning eyes, loss of smell, night blindness, rough dry skin, sinus trouble, soft tooth enamel, susceptibility to infection.

Therapeutic Application
Acne, alcoholism, allergies, arthritis, asthma, athletes foot, bronchitis, colds, cystitis, diabetes, eczema, heart disease, hepatitis, migraine headaches, psoriasis.

B COMPLEX

Water Soluble

Complementing Nutrients
C, E, calcium, phosphorus

Anti-Vitamins
Alcohol, birth control pills, coffee, infections, sleeping pills, stress, sugar (excessive), sulfa drugs.

Sources
Brewer's yeast, liver, whole grains, green leafy vegetables

Bodily Parts Affected
Eyes, gastrointestinal tract, hair, liver, mouth, nerves, skin.

Bodily Functions Facilitated
Energy, metabolism, (carbohydrate, fat, protein), muscle tone maintenance (gastrointestinal tract).

Deficiency Symtoms
Acne, anemia, constipation, cholesterol (high), digestive disturbances, fatigue, hair (dull, dry, falling), insomnia, skin (dry, rough).

Therapeutic Applications
Alcoholic psychosis, allergies, anemia, baldness, barbituate overdose, cystitis, heart abnormalities, hypoglycemia, hypersensitve children, menstrual difficulties, migraine headaches, overweight, postoperative nausea, stress.

B1 (Thiamine)

Water Soluble

Complementing Nutrients
B complex*, B2, folic acid, niacin, C, E, manganese, sulphur.

Anti-Vitamins
Alcohol, coffee, fever, raw clams, sugar (excessive), stress, surgery, tobacco.

Sources
Blackstrap molasses, brewer's yeast, brown rice, fish, meat, nuts, organ meats, poultry, wheat germ.

Brewer's yeast - 2 tbsp.	3 mg.
Peanuts - 1¼ cups	1 mg.
Sunflower seeds - 1 cup	2 mg.
Brazil nuts - 1 cup	3 mg.

Bodily Parts Affected
Brain, ears, eyes, hair, heart, nervous system.

Bodily Functions Facilitated
Appetite, blood building, carbohydrate metabolism, circulation, digestion (hydrochloric acid production), energy, growth, learning capacity, muscle tone maintenance (intestines, stomach, heart).

Deficiency Symptoms
Appetite loss, digestive disturbances, fatigue, irritability, nervousness, numbness of hands & feet, pain & noise sensitivity, pain around heart, shortness of breath.

Therapeutic Applications

Alcoholism, anemia, congestive heart failure, constipation, diarrhea, indigestion, nausea, mental illness, rapid heart rate, stress, pain (alleviation).

B2 (Riboflavin)

Water Soluble

Complementing Nutrients
B complex*, B6**, niacin, C, phosphorus.

Anti-Vitamins
Alcohol, coffee, sugar (excessive), tobacco.

Sources
Blackstrap molasses, nuts, organ meats, whole grains.

Almonds - 1 cup	1 mg.
Brussel sprouts - 1 cup	2 mg.
Brewer's yeast - 3 tbsp.	1 mg.
Liver (beef) - ¼ lb.	5 mg.

Bodily Parts Affected
Eyes, hair, nails, skin, soft body tissue.

Bodily Functions Facilitated
Antibody & red blood cell formation, cell respiration, metabolism (carbohydrate, fat, protein).

Deficiency Symtoms
Cataracts, corner of mouth cracks & sores, dizziness, itching, burning eyes, poor digestion, retarded growth, red sore tongue.

Therapeutic Applications
Acne, alcoholism, arthritis, athletes foot, baldness, cataracts, diabetes, diarrhea, indigestion, stress.

B6 (Pyridoxine)

Water Soluble

Complementing Nutrients
B complex*, B1, B2, pantothenic acid, C, magnesium, potassium, linoleic acid, sodium.

Anti-Vitamins
Alcohol, birth control pills, coffee, radiation (exposure), tobacco.

Sources
Blackstrap molasses, brewer's yeast, green leafy vegetables, meat, organ meats, wheat germ, whole grains, desiccated liver.

Liver (beef) - ¼ lb.	1 mg.
Prunes (cooked) - 1 cup	2 mg.
Brown rice - 1 cup	2 mg.
Peas - 1 cup	2 mg.

Bodily Parts Affected
Blood, muscles, nerves, skin.

Bodily Functions Facilitated
Antibody formation, digestion (hydrochloric acid production), fat and protein utilization (weight control), sodium potassium balance (nerves).

Deficiency Symtoms
Acne, anemia, arthritis, convulsions in infants, depression, dizziness, hair loss, irritability, learning disabilities, weakness.

Therapeutic Applications
Arteriosclerosis, baldness, cholesterol (high), cystitis, facial oiliness, hyperglycemia, mental retardation, muscular disorders, nausea in pregnancy, sun sensitivity, post operative nausea, stress, overweight, nervous disorders.

B12 (Cobalamin)

Water Soluble

Complementing Nutrients
B complex*, B6*, choline, Inositol, C, Potassium, sodium.

Anti-Vitamins
Alcohol, coffee, laxatives, tobacco.

Sources
Cheese, fish, milk, milk products, organ meats,

Cottage cheese - 1 cup	2 mcg.
Liver (beef) - ¼ lb.	90 mcg.
Tuna fish (canned) - ¼ lb.	5 mcg.
Eggs - 1 med.	1 mcg.
Milk - 1 cup	1 mcg.

Bodily Parts Affected
Blood, nerves.

Bodily Functions Facilitated
Appetite, blood cell formation, cell longevity, healthy nervous system, metabolism (carbohydrate, fat, protein).

Deficiency Symptoms
General weakness, nervousness, pernicious anemia, walking & speaking difficulty.

Therapeutic Application
Alcoholism, allergies, anemia, arthritis, bronchial asthma, bursitis, epilepsy, fatigue, hypoglycemia, insomnia, overweight, shingles, stress.

BIOTIN (B complex)

Water Soluble

Complementing Nutrients
B complex*, B 12, folic acid, panthothenic acid, C, sulphur.

Anti-Vitamin
Alcohol, coffee, raw egg white (avidin).

Sources
Legumes, whole grains, organ meats.

Brewer's yeast - 1 tbsp.	20 mcg.
Lentils - 1 cup	25 mcg.
Mungbean sprouts - 1 cup	200 mcg.
Egg yolk - 1 med.	10 mcg.
Liver (beef) - ¼ lb.	112 mcg.
Soy beans - 1 cup	120 mcg.

Bodily Parts Affected
Hair, muscles, skin.

Bodily Functions Facilitated
Cell growth, fatty acid production, metabolism (carbo-hydrate, fat, protein), vitamin B utilization.

Deficiency Symptoms
Depression, dry skin, fatigue, grayish skin color, insomnia, muscular pain, poor appetite.

Therapeutic Application
Baldness, dermatitis, eczema, leg cramps.

CHOLINE (B complex)

Water soluble

Complementing Nutrients
A, B complex, B12, folic acid, inositol*, linoleic acid.

Anti-Vitamins
Alcohol, coffee, sugar (excessive).

Source
Brewer's yeast, fish, legumes, organ meats, soy beans, wheatgerm, lecithin.

Liver (beef) - ¼ lb.	500 mcg.
Egg yolk - 1 med.	250 mcg.
Peanuts (roasted w/skin) - ½ cup	190 mcg.

Bodily Parts Affected
Hair, kidneys, liver, thymus gland.

Bodily Functions Facilitated
Lecithin formation, liver & gall bladder regulation, metabolism (fats, cholesterol), nerve transmission.

Deficiency Symtoms
Bleeding stomach ulcers, growth problems, heart trouble, high blood pressure, impaired liver & kidney function, intolerance to fats.

Therapeutic Applications
Alcoholism, arteriosclerosis, baldness, cholesterol (high), constipation, dizziness, ear noises, hardening of the arteries, headaches, heart trouble, high blood pressure, hypoglycemia, insomnia.

FOLIC ACID (folacin B complex)

Water Soluble

Complementing Nutrients
B complex*, B12*, biotin, Pantothenic acid, C.

Anti-Vitamin
Alcohol, coffee, stress, tobacco.

Source
Green leafy vegetables, milk, milk products, organ meats,
oysters, salmon, whole grains.

Brewer's yeast - 1 tbsp.	200 mcg.
Dates (dried) - 1 med.	2,500 mcg.
Spinach (steamed) - 1 cup	448 mcg.
Tuna fish (canned) - ¼ lb.	2,500 mcg.

Bodily Parts Affected
Blood, glands, liver.

Bodily Functions Facilitated
Appetite, body growth & reproduction, hydrochloric acid
production, protein metabolism, red blood cell formation.

Deficiency Symtoms
Anemia, digestive disturbances, graying hair, growth
problems.

Therapeutic Applications
Alcoholism, anemia, arteriosclerosis, baldness, diarrhea,
fatigue, menstrual problems, mental illness, stomach
ulcers, stress.

INOSITOL (B complex)

Water Soluble

Complementing Nutrients
B complex*, B12, choline*, linoleic acid.

Anti-Vitamins
Alcohol, coffee.

Source
Blackstrap molasses, citrus fruits, brewer's yeast, meat, milk, nuts, vegetables, whole grains, lecithin.

Orange (fresh) - 1 med.   400 mg.
Grapefruit - 1 med.   500 mg.
Peanuts (roasted w/skin)
½ cup   400 mg.

Bodily Parts Affected
Brain, hair, heart, kidneys, liver, muscles.

Bodily Functions Facilitated
Artery hardening retardation, cholesterol reduction, hair growth, lecithin formation, metabolism (fat & cholesterol).

Deficiency Symtoms
Cholesterol (high), constipation, eczema, eye abnormalities, hair loss.

Therapeutic Applications
Arteriosclerosis, baldness, cholesterol (high), constipation, heart disease, overweight.

NIACIN (Niacinamide, B complex)

Water Soluble

Complementing Nutrients
B complex*, B1, B2, C, phosphorus*.

Anti-Vitamin
Alcohol, antibiotics, coffee, corn, sugar/starches (excessive).

Sources
Brewer's yeast, seafood, lean meats, milk, milk products, poultry, desiccated liver.

rhubarb (cooked)	80 mg.
chicken (breast fried) ½ lb.	25 mg.
peanuts (roasted w/skin) 1 cup	40 mg.

Bodily Parts Affected
Brain, liver, nerves, skin, soft tissue, tongue.

Bodily Parts Facilitated
Circulation, cholesterol level reduction, growth, hydrochloric acid production, metabolism (protein, fat, carbohydrate), sex hormone production.

Deficiency Symptoms
Appetite loss, canker sores, depression, fatigue, halitosis, headaches, indigestion, insomnia, muscular weakness, nausea, nervous disorders, skin eruptions.

Therapeutic Applications
Acne, baldness, diarrhea, halitosis, high blood pressure, leg cramps, migraine headaches, poor circulation, stress.

PANGAMIC ACID (B15)

Water Soluble

Complementing Nutrients
B complex*, C, E.

Anti-Vitamins
Alcohol, coffee.

Sources
Brewer's yeast, brown rice, meat (rare), seeds (sunflower, sesame, pumpkin), whole grains, organ meats.

Bodily Parts Affected
Glands, heart, kidneys, nerves.

Bodily Functions Facilitated
Cell oxidation & respiration, metabolism (protein, fat, sugar), glandular & nervous system stimulation.

Deficiency Symptoms
Heart disease, nervous & glandular disorders.

Therapeutic Applications
Alcoholism, asthma, arteriosclerosis, cholesterol (high), emphysema, heart disease, headaches, insomnia, poor circulation, premature aging, rheumatism, shortness of breath.

PANTOTHENIC ACID (B complex)

Water Soluble

Complementing Nutrients
B complex*, B6, B12, biotin, folic acid, C.

Anti-Vitamins
Alcohol, coffee.

Sources
Brewer's yeast, legumes, organ meats, salmon, wheat germ, whole grains.

Liver (beef) - ¼ lb.	8 mg.
Mushrooms (cooked) - 1 cup	25 mg.
Elderberries (raw) - 1 cup	82 mg.
Orange juice (fresh) - 1 cup	45 mg.

Bodily Parts Affected
Adrenal glands, digestive tract, nerves, skin.

Bodily Functions Facilitated
Antibody formation, carbohydrate, fat, protein conversion (energy), growth stimulation, vitamin utilization.

Deficiency Symtoms
Diarrhea, duodenal ulcers, eczema, hypoglycemia, intestinal disorders, kidney trouble, loss of hair, muscle cramps, premature aging, respiratory infections, restlessness, nerve problems, sore feet, vomiting.

Therapeutic Applications
Allergies, arthritis, baldness, cystitis, digestive disorders, hypoglycemia, tooth decay, stress.

PARA AMINOBENSOIC ACID
(paba, B complex)

Water Soluble

Complementing Nutrients
B complex*, folic acid, C.

Anti-Vitamins
Alcohol, coffee, sulfa drugs.

Sources
Blackstrap molasses, brewer's yeast, liver, organ meats, wheat germ.

Bodily Parts Affected
Glands, hair, intestines, skin.

Bodily Functions Facilitated
Blood cell formation, graying hair (color restoration), intestinal bacteria activity, protein metabolism.

Deficiency Symptoms
Constipation, depression, digestive disorders, fatigue, gray hair, headaches, irritability.

Therapeutic Application
Baldness, graying hair, overactive thyroid gland, parasitic diseases, rheumatic fever, stress, infertility, dark skin spots, dry skin, sunburn, wrinkles.

C (Ascorbic acid)

Water Soluble

Complementing Nutrients
All vitamins & minerals, bioflavonoids, calcuim*, magnesium*.

Anti-Vitamins
Antibiotics, aspirin, cortisone, high fever, stress, tobacco.

Sources
Citrus fruits, cantaloupe, green peppers.

Broccoli (cooked) - 1 cup	135 mg.
Oranges - 1 med.	100 mg.
Peppers (green) - 1 med.	120 mg.
Grapefruit - 1 med.	100 mg.
Papaya (raw) - 1 lg.	225 mg.
Strawberries - 1 cup	90 mg.

Bodily Parts Affected
Adrenal glands, blood capillary walls, connective tissue (skin, ligaments, bones), gums, heart, teeth.

Body Functions Facilitated
Bone & tooth formation, collagen production, digestion, iodine conservation, healing (burns & wounds), red blood cell formation (hemorrhaging prevention), shock & infection resistance (colds), vitamin production (oxidation).

Deficiency Symptoms
Anemia, bleeding gums, capillary wall ruptures, bruise easily, dental cavities, low infection resistance (colds), nosebleeds, poor digestion.

Therapeutic Applications
Alcoholism, allergies, arteriosclerosis, arthritis, baldness, cholesterol (high), colds, cystitis, hypoglycemia, heart disease, hepatitis, insect bites, overweight, prickly heat, sinusitis, stress, tooth decay.

D

Fat Soluble

Complementing Nutrients
A, choline, C, F, calcium, phosphorus.

Anti-Vitamins
Mineral oil.

Sources
Egg yolks, organ meats, bone meal, sunlight.

Liver (beef) - ¼ lb.	40 IU
Milk, - 1 cup	100 IU
Salmon, tuna (canned) - ¼ lb.	300 IU

Bodily Parts Affected
Bones, heart, nerves, skin, teeth, thyroid gland.

Bodily Functions Facilitated
Calcium & phosphorus, metabolism (bone formation), heart action, nervous system maintenance, normal blood clotting, skin respiration.

Deficiency Symptoms
Burning sensation (mouth & throat), diarrhea, insomnia, myopia, nervousness, poor metabolism, softening bones & teeth.

Therapeutic Applications
Acne, alcoholism, allergies, arthritis, cystitis, eczema, psoriasis, stress.

E (Tocopherol)

Fat Soluble

Complementing Nutrients
A, B complex, B1, inositol*, C, F, manganese*, selenium, phosphorus*.

Anti-Vitamins
Birth control pills, chlorine, mineral oil, rancid fat & oil.

Sources
Dark green vegetables, eggs, liver, organ meats, wheatgerm, vegetable oils, desiccated liver.

Oatmeal (cooked) - 1 cup	7 IU
Safflower oil, - 1 tbsp.	20 IU
Vegetable oils, - 1 tbsp.	12 IU
Peanuts (roasted w/skin) - 1 cup	13 IU
Tomatoes, 2 med.	3 UI
Wheatgerm oil, - 1 tbsp.	40 IU

Bodily Parts Affected
Blood vessels, heart, lungs, nerves, pituitary gland, skin.

Bodily Functions Facilitated
Aging retardation, anti-clotting factor, blood cholesterol reduction, blood flow to heart, capillary wall strenghening, fertility, male potency, lung protection, (anti-pollution), muscle & nerve maintenance.

Deficiency Symptoms
Dry, dull, or falling hair; enlarged prostate gland; gastro-

intestinal disease; heart disease; impotency; miscarriages; muscular wasting; sterility.

Therapeutic Application

Allergies, arthritis, arteriosclerosis, baldness, cholesterol (high), crossed eyes, cystitis, diabetes, heart disease (coronary thrombosis, angina pectoris, rheumatic heart disease), menstrual problems, menopause, migraine headaches, myopia, overweight, phebitis, sinusitis, stress, thrombosis, burns, varicose veins, scars, warts, wrinkles.

F (Unsaturated Fatty Acids)

Fat Soluble

Complementing Nutrients
A, C, D, E, phosphorus

Anti-Vitamins
Radiation, x-rays

Sources
Vegetable oils (safflower, soy, corn), wheat germ, sunflower seeds.

Bodily Parts Affected
Cells, glands (adrenal, thyroid), hair mucous membranes, nerves, skin.

Bodily Functions Facilitated
Artery hardening prevention, blood coagulation, blood pressure normalizer, cholesterol destroyer, glandular activity, growth, vital organ respiration.

Deficiency Symptoms
Acne, allergies, diarrhea, dry skin, dry brittle hair, eczema, gall stones, nail problems, underweight, varicose veins.

Therapeutic Applications
Allergies, baldness, bronchial asthma, cholesterol (high), eczema, gallbladder problems or removal, heart disease, leg ulcers, psoriasis, rheumatoid arthritis, overweight, underweight.

K (Menadione)

Fat soluble

Complementing Nutrients
Unknown

Anti-Vitamins
Aspirin, antibiotics (excessive), mineral oil, radiation, rancid fats, x-ray.

Sources
Green leafy vegetables, safflower oil, blackstrap molasses, yogurt.

Oatmeal - 1 cup	180 mcg.
Liver (beef) - ¼ lb.	100 mcg.

Bodily Parts Affected
Blood, liver.

Bodily Functions Facilitated
Blood clotting (coagulation).

Deficiency Symptoms
Diarrhea, increased tendency to hemorrhage, miscarriages, nosebleeds.

Therapeutic Applications
Bruising, eye hemorrhages, gall stones, hemmorrhaging menstrual problems, preparing women for childbirth.

P (Bioflavonoids)

Water Soluble

Complementing Nutrients
Vitamin C.

Anti-Vitamins
See vitamin C above, especially tendency to bleed and bruise easily.

Sources
Fruits (skins & pulps), apricots, cherries, grapes, grapefruit, lemons, plums.

Bodily Parts Affected
Blood, capillary walls, connective tissue (skin) gums, ligaments, bones), teeth.

Bodily Functions Facilitated
Blood vessel wall maintenance, bruising minimization, cold & flu prevention, strong capillary maintenance.

Deficiency Symptoms
See Vitamin C above.

Therapeutic Application
Asthma, bleeding gums, colds, eczema, dizziness (caused by inner ear) hemorrhoids, high blood pressure, miscarriages, rheumatic fever, rheumatism, ulcers.

CALCIUM

Complementing Nutrients
A*, C*, D*, F. iron*, magnesium, manganese, phosphorus*.

Anti-Minerals
Lack of exercise, stress (excessive).

Source
Milk, cheese, molasses, yogurt, bone meal, dolomite.

Almonds - 1 cup	325 mg.
American cheese - 1 slice	200 mg.
Liver (beef) - ¼ lb.	500 mg.

Bodily Part Affected
Blood, bones, heart, skin, soft tissue, teeth.

Bodily Functions Facilitated
Bone, tooth formation, blood clotting, heart rhythm, nerve tranqualization, nerve transmission, muscle growth & contraction.

Deficiency Symptoms
Heart palpitations, insomnia, muscle cramps, nervousness, arm & leg numbness, tooth decay.

Therapeutic Application
Arthritis, aging symptoms (backache, bone pain, finger tremors), foot/leg cramps, insomnia, menstrual cramps, menopause problems, nervousness, overweight, pre-menstrual tension, rheumatism.

CHROMIUM

Complementing Nutrients
None

Anti-Minerals
None

Sources
Brewer's yeast, clams, corn oil, whole grain cereals.

Bodily Parts Affected
Blood, circulatory system.

Bodily Functions Facilitated
Blood sugar level, glugose metabolism (energy).

Deficiency Symptoms
Arteriosclerosis, glucose intolerance in diabetics.

Therapeutic Applications
Diabetes, hypoglycemia.

COPPER

Complementing Nutrients
Cobalt, iron, zinc.

Anti-Minerals
Zinc (high intakes).

Sources
Legumes, nuts, organ meats, seafood, raisins, molasses, bone meal.

Brazil nuts - 1 cup	4 mg.
Soybeans - 1 cup	2 mg.

Bodily Parts Affected
Blood, bones, circulatory system, hair, skin.

Bodily Functions Facilitated
Bone formation, hair & skin color, healing processes of body, hemoglobin & red blood cell formation.

Deficiency Symptoms
General weakness, impaired respiration, skin sores.

Therapeutic Applications
Anemia, baldness.

IODINE

Complementing Nutrients
None

Anti-Minerals
None

Sources
Seafood, kelp tablets, salt (iodized).

Bodily Parts Affected
Hair, nails, skin, teeth, thyroid gland.

Bodily Functions Facilitated
Energy production, metabolism (excess fat), physical & mental development.

Deficiency Symptoms
Cold hands & feet, dry hair, irritability, nervousness, obesity.

Therapeutic Application
Arteriosclerosis, hair problems, goiter, hyperthyroidism.

IRON

Complementing Nutrients
B12, folic acid, C*, calcium*, cobalt, copper*, phosphorus.

Anti-Minerals
Coffee, excess phosphorus, tea, zinc (excessive intake).

Sources
Blackstrap molasses, eggs, fish, organ meats, poultry, wheat germ, desiccated liver.

Liver (beef) - ¼ lb.	200 mg.
Shredded wheat - 1 biscuit	30 mg.

Bodily Parts Affected
Blood, bones, nails, skin, teeth.

Bodily Functions Facilitated
Hemoglobin production, stress & desease resistance.

Deficiency Symptoms
Breathing difficulties, brittle nails, iron deficiency anemia (pale skin, fatigue), constipation.

Therapeutic Applications
Alcoholism, anemia, colitis, menstrual problems.

MAGNESIUM

Complementing Nutrients
B6*, C, D, calcium, phosphorus.

Anti-Minerals
None

Sources
Bran, honey, green vegetables, nuts, seafood, spinach, bone meal, kelp tablets.

Bran flakes - 1 cup	90 mg.
Peanuts, (roasted w/skin) - 1 cup	420 mg.
Tuna fish, (canned) - ½ lb.	150 mg.

Bodily Parts Affected
Arteries, bones, heart, muscles, nerves, teeth.

Bodily Functions Facilitated
Acid/alkaline balance, blood sugar metabolism (energy), metabolism (calcium & vitamin C).

Deficiency Symptoms
Confusion, disorientation, easily aroused anger, nervousness, rapid pulse, tremors.

Therapeutic Applications
Alcoholism, cholesterol (high) depression, heart conditions, kidney stones, nervousness, prostate troubles, sensitivity to noise, stomach acidity, tooth decay, overweight.

MANGANESE

Complementing Nutrients
None

Anti-Minerals
Calcium/phosphorus (excessive intake).

Sources
Bananas, bran, celery, cereals, egg yolks, green leafy vegetables, legumes, liver, nuts, pinapples, whole grains.

Bodily Parts Affected
Brain, mammary glands, muscles, nerves.

Bodily Functions Facilitated
Enzyme activation, reproduction & growth, sex hormone production, tissue respiration, vitamin B1 metabolism, vitamin E utilization.

Deficiency Symptoms
Ataxia (muscle coordination failure), dizziness, ear noises, loss of hearing.

Therapeutic Applications
Allergies, asthma, diabetes, fatigue.

PHOSPHORUS

Complementing Nutrients
A, D*, F, calcium**, iron, manganese.

Anti-Minerals
Aluminum, iron, magnesium (excessive intake), white sugar (excessive).

Sources
Eggs, fish, grains, glandular meats, meat, poultry, yellow cheese.

Calf liver - ¼ lb.	600 mg.
Milk/ yogurt - 1 cup	230 mg.
Eggs (cooked) - 1 med.	110 mg.

Bodily Parts Affected
Bones, brain, nerves, teeth.

Bodily Functions Facilitated
Bone, tooth formation, cell growth & repair, energy production, heart muscle contraction, kidney function, metabolism (calcium sugar), nerve & muscle activity, vitamin utilization.

Deficiency Symptoms
Appetite loss, fatigue, irregular breathing, nervous disorders, overweight, weightloss.

Therapeutic Applications
Arthritis, stunted growth in children, stress, tooth & gum disorders.

POTASSIUM

Complementing Nutrients
B6, sodium**.

Anti-Minerals
Alcohol, coffee, cortisone, diuretics, laxatives, salt (excessive), sugar (excessive), stress.

Sources
Dates, figs, peaches, tomato juice, blackstrap molasses, peanuts, raisins, seafood.

Apricots (dried) - 1 cup	1,450 mg.
Bananas - 1 med.	500 mg.
Flounder (baked) - ¼ lb.	650 mg.
Potatoes (baked) - 1 med.	500 mg.
Sunflower seeds - 1 cup	900 mg.

Bodily Parts Affected
Blood, heart, kidneys, muscles, nerves, skin.

Bodily Functions Facilitated
Heartbeat, rapid growth, muscle contraction, nerve tranquilization.

Deficiency Symptoms
Acne, continuous thirst, dry skin, constipation, general weakness, insomnia, muscle damage, nervousness, slow irregular heartbeat, weak reflexes.

Therapeutic Application
Acne, alcoholism, allergies, burns, colic in infants, diabetes, high blood pressure, heart disease (angina pectoris, congestive heart failure, myocardial infarction).

SODIUM

Complementing Nutrients
D, Potassium.

Anti-Minerals
Chlorine, potassium (lack of).

Source
Salt, milk, cheese, seafood.

Bodily Parts Affected
Blood, lymph system, muscles, nerves.

Bodily Functions Facilitated
Normal cellular fluid level, proper muscle contracation.

Deficiency Symptoms
Appetite loss, intestinal gas, muscle shrinkage, vomiting, weight loss.

Therapeutic Applications
Dehydration, fever, heat stroke.

SULPHUR

Complementing Nutrients
B complex, B1, biotin, pantothenic acid.

Anti-Minerals
None

Sources
Bran, cheese, clams, eggs, nuts, fish, wheat germ.

Bodily Parts Affected
Hair, nails, nerves, skin.

Bodily Functions Facilitated
Collagen synthesis, body tissue formation.

Deficiency Symptoms
Unknown

Therapeutic Applications
Arthritis, skin disorders (eczema, dermatitis, psoriasis).

ZINC

Complementing Nutrients
A, calcium, copper, phosphorus.

Anti-Minerals
Alcohol, calcium (high intake), phosphorus (lack of).

Sources
Brewer's yeast, liver, seafood, soybeans, spinach, sunflower seeds, mushrooms.

Bodily Parts Affected
Blood, heart, prostate gland.

Bodily Functions Facilitated
Burn & wound healing, carbohydrate digestion, prostate gland function, reproductive organ growth & development, sex organ growth & maturity, vitamin B1, phosphorus & protein metabolism.

Deficiency Symptoms
Delayed sexual maturity, fatigue, loss of taste, poor appetite, prolonged wound healing, retarded growth, sterility.

Therapeutic Applications
Alcoholism, arteriosclerosis, baldness, cirrhosis, diabetes, internal & external wound & injury healing, high cholesterol (eliminates deposits) infertility.

INDEX

DO A FRIEND A FAVOR - Order a book for a gift. Use the convenient Order Form below.

- -

Send to:
CRAB COVE BOOKS
P.O. Box 214
Alameda, Ca. 94501

Please send me _____ copies of *MY HOUSE TO YOURS*.

I am enclosing $_____ (check or money order). No CODs. Please send $9.95 plus $2.00 shipping & handling for each book. (Californians add applicable tax.) Price is subject to change without notice.

PLEASE PRINT OR TYPE

Name _____

Address _____

City _____ State _____ Zip Code _____

Allow up to 4 weeks for delivery.

- -

- -

Send to:
CRAB COVE BOOKS
P.O. Box 214
Alameda, Ca. 94501

Please send me _____ copies of *MY HOUSE TO YOURS*.

I am enclosing $_____ (check or money order). No CODs. Please send $9.95 plus $2.00 shipping & handling for each book. (Californians add applicable tax.) Price is subject to change without notice.

PLEASE PRINT OR TYPE

Name _____

Address _____

City _____ State _____ Zip Code _____

Allow up to 4 weeks for delivery.

- -